"Our souls long for the help offered in these pages: learning how to connect the dots for developing an integrated and permeable soul based on our truest relationship with the triune God of love and a deeply trusting quality of relationships with others. I highly recommend reading and reflecting on this life-giving content offered by two trustworthy professionals. You will dog-ear many pages to reference in your personal journey toward genuine transformation."

Stephen Macchia, president of Leadership Transformations, author of *Crafting a Rule of Life*

"I am delighted that Rich has (at long last) put his considerable wisdom into a book. His understanding of relationships has brought me significant help. Rich and Jim call themselves 'wounded writers.' As such they are the best kind of guides for teaching us about vulnerability and connection. Their biblical and psychological integration creates hope for wholeness and health."

Adele Calhoun, author of *The Spiritual Disciplines Handbook* and *Invitations from God*

"*The Relational Soul* provides real insight into why relationships are so essential, and yet often so aching. Coauthors Plass and Cofield provide practical helps for self-discovery and communion with God that will deepen your relationships with God and others. Hope and help for healing is here!"

Mindy Caliguire, Willow Creek Association

"Richard Plass and James Cofield's *The Relational Soul* is an engaging explication of the fact that as humans we are created in the image of a trinitarian God who exists in a loving, relational community. It is also a needed reminder of how people are both hurt and healed through the relational fabric of existence."

Gary W. Moon, executive director of the Martin Institute and Dallas Willard Center, Westmont College, and author of *Apprenticeship with Jesus*

"You are holding in your hands more than a book. Richard Plass and James Cofield have given us a roadmap to help us find the way to each other and to the heart of God. Beautifully written, masterfully developed and applicable for those who want true community but have not tasted it yet, this book helps us find our way to each other in an age of isolation, loneliness and existence in silos where we survive but we do not thrive. Here's to thriving!"

Stephen W. Smith, president and spiritual director of Potter's Inn Ministry, author of *The Lazarus Life* and *The Jesus Life*

"There are far too many books, both secular and spiritual, for 'coached' living. Finally, Plass and Cofield have penned the needed depth in who and what we are to face ourselves before God—thus allowing God's full, redemptive grace to be what it should in our relationships. The stories are real, the writing terse and piercing. My humble counsel is get it, read it, mark it up, use it and pass it on—if you can let it

go—because you will want to refer to this time and time again. It's that good."
M. L. Hillard, senior vice president, Peter F. Drucker Academy, Beijing

"What a joy to read this distillation of the union of two lifetimes of journeying with Christ into greater communion with God and others. Whether we are aware of it or not, we spend the early phase of our adulthood seeking to conform our worlds to the template of our earliest attachments and the self we became in those relationships. Rich and Jim have engagingly described how relational renewal in Christ can change that template, as we learn how to trust him to make us the kind of people who can receive it."
Eric L. Johnson, professor of pastoral care, The Southern Baptist Theological Seminary, and director, Society for Christian Psychology

"I found Jim and Rich's work in *The Relational Soul* to be both provocative and encouraging. It elicited a deep longing to know myself better and connect in lifegiving relationships with others, especially God. Jim and Rich have awakened a desire for this 'narrow way' of profound relational connection. I'm grateful!
Dave Rodriguez, senior pastor, Grace Church, Noblesville, Indiana

"In a culture where keystrokes are being confused for relationships, Jim and Rich provide an insightful look at how God created us for real connection that begins with our souls. We have been the beneficiaries of wisdom, spiritual direction and relational clarity from a long friendship with Jim and Rich and are delighted to now have their wisdom captured in this book. If you long to grow in the art of self-care, deepened relationships with others and intimacy with God, this book is for you."
Jeff and Lora Helton, coauthors of *The Fifty Fridays Marriage Challenge*

"Jim Cofield and Rich Plass are a gift to the church. These men and the content in this book were God's means to save my life and ministry after severe burnout. Drawing on the riches of God's common grace and special grace, *The Relational Soul* provides what is lacking in much of modern spiritual formation. Your soul will be better off if you take seriously the content of these pages."
Harvey Turner, founding and preaching pastor of Living Stones Church, network director of Acts 29 West

"*The Relational Soul* teaches us how to be present to God and present to others—in our marriages, in our homes, in our ministries and in our entire lives. Plass and Cofield blaze a trail, not only for pastors and leaders who are beat-up and burned out, but for all followers of Christ to rediscover their first love. This book is an effective tool to help guide and direct us back to the soul-changing good news found in Jesus Christ. I'm personally thankful for these two gospel wizards, Plass and Cofield, and the gospel magic that they perform. Their fresh insights and encouragements are hope for us all."
Daniel Montgomery, pastor, Sojourn Community Church

The
RELATIONAL
SOUL

*Moving from False Self
to Deep Connection*

*RICHARD PLASS
and JAMES COFIELD*

IVP Books

An imprint of InterVarsity Press
Downers Grove, Illinois

InterVarsity Press
P.O. Box 1400, Downers Grove, IL 60515-1426
www.ivpress.com
email@ivpress.com

InterVarsity Press˚ is the book-publishing division of InterVarsity Christian Fellowship/USA˚, a movement of students and faculty active on campus at hundreds of universities, colleges and schools of nursing in the United States of America, and a member movement of the International Fellowship of Evangelical Students. For information about local and regional activities, write Public Relations Dept., InterVarsity Christian Fellowship/USA, 6400 Schroeder Rd., P.O. Box 7895, Madison, WI 53707-7895, or visit the IVCF website at www.intervarsity.org.

Unless otherwise indicated, all Scripture quotations are taken from the Holy Bible, New Living Translation, copyright ©1996, 2004. Used by permission of Tyndale House Publishers, Inc., Wheaton, Illinois 60189. All rights reserved.

While all stories in this book are true, some names and identifying information in this book have been changed to protect the privacy of the individuals involved.

Cover design: Cindy Kiple
Interior design: Beth Hagenberg
Images: yellow texture: ©hudlemm/iStockphoto
*   still life: ©Elisabeth Ansley/Trevillion Images*

ISBN 978-0-8308-3587-4 (print)
ISBN 978-0-8308-9651-6 (digital)

Printed in the United States of America ∞

Library of Congress Cataloging-in-Publication Data

A catalog record for this book is available from the Library of Congress.

P	18	17	16	15	14	13	12	11	10	9	8	7	6	5	4	3	2	1
Y	29	28	27	26	25	24	23	22	21	20	19	18	17	16	15	14		

We could not have written this book
without the loving and life-giving presence of our wives.
Through them we have learned to trust more fully
and thus relate more deeply. We dedicate
this book to them, Sallie and Joy.

Our children have also taught and helped us
in ways they cannot know.

Rich:

To my children, Jennifer, Rebekah, Elisabeth
(and their husbands Troy, Ben and Chris),
Margaret, Matthew and Michelle,
I say thank you.

Jim:

To my children, Justin (and his wife Kristina)
and Ashley, I also say thank you.

CONTENTS

1

Our Relational Reality

Created for Connecting

*H*arry lived directly across the road from my (Rich) house in upstate New York. He was alone in his midnineteenth-century farmhouse, which was barely hanging on to its earlier days of beauty. Harry would occasionally eat dinner with our family, paying my mother four or five dollars a week for his meals. His claim to fame at our dinner table was pouring chicken gravy on my mother's homemade apple pie. How that tasted I'm not sure; I never tried it!

One night when I was twelve years old I woke up frightened out of my wits. It sounded as if someone was kicking in the front door, which was immediately below my bedroom. I heard my father jump out of bed and head down the stairs, muttering things I cannot repeat here. Opening the door he came face to face with Harry. Harry barged into our front room, settled into a yawning floral blue chair without a word and in a matter of minutes was sound asleep. My father climbed the stairs still muttering pretty much what he did on the way down. By 6 a.m. Harry had disappeared back into his old farmhouse.

Harry's midnight episodes continued over the next six months. He routinely woke up my family by pounding on the door. Each time my father muttered as he headed down the stairs to let Harry into the front room, where Harry slept until early morning. These episodes stopped when Harry was taken to the hospital. My mother told me he was terminally ill with cancer. Several weeks later Harry died alone.

Many things struck me about Harry. There was the thing about pouring gravy on apple pie. And there was his beating on our door in the middle of the night. But what made even more of an impression on me was his loneliness, which was evident even to me as a young boy. Some evenings Harry would sit on the front steps of his farmhouse with his German shepherd next to him. Occasionally, I crossed the road and asked Harry how he was doing. He always answered, "Pretty good." But I knew he was sad, because the conversation never went much further. At that point I would throw sticks for the dog to retrieve while Harry watched. At dusk Father would whistle or Mother would call, and I would head home. When I said, "Night," Harry would raise his hand with a gentle wave. But he remained silent.

Harry's loneliness had its own story line. He was divorced before my parents built their house across the road from his farm in 1933. He hung on to the memory of better days through an empty old house that, by size and design, signaled a time when conversation and personal connection was something real. When I knew him, his house was the only connection to others who mattered most to him. Its dilapidated condition mirrored the sadness of his alienation from his former wife and only son, connections that had been lost for years.

Harry never found his way toward reconciliation, and consequently he lived with unresolved pain unknown to others and mostly disowned by himself. He never really understood his own soul or a way toward life-giving communion. He settled for what was available—the companionship of a dog, the kid who lived across the road, a night out here and there, and chicken gravy on homemade apple pie. He tolerated his loneliness until his end was in sight. At that point his way of coping no longer worked. In his final months he could not help but pound on our front door in the middle of the night in a desperate attempt to find some relief through distant connection.

OUR RELATIONAL LIFE

Harry didn't vote for loneliness. But that is where he found himself. And that is where many of us find ourselves. Hopefully, we are not as desperate as Harry was. But many have experienced an inner void that fosters anxiety over the empty places in our souls. "Practically every human being . . . has experienced that strange inner gnawing, that mental hunger, that unsettling unrest that makes us say, 'I feel lonely.' Loneliness is one of the most universal experiences."[1]

Loneliness is "the broad way" that many of us travel. We develop ways to cope with its sadness, ways to manage its pain, ways to exist with its emptiness. But the longer we live, the greater the chance we will find ourselves in deep shadows where the darkness proves difficult to bear. Like Harry, we wind up "knocking on a door."

What does loneliness tell us about ourselves? Be it chronic or acute, slight or significant, loneliness is proof of our rela- tional design. At the core of our being is this truth—*we are designed* for *and defined* by *our relationships.* We were born with a relentless longing to participate in the lives of others. Fundamentally, we are relational souls. We cannot *not* be re- lational. In fact, all of our knowing is interpersonal in that it emerges from a soul that is structured relationally.[2] We cannot exist well without connection and communion with another. Relational reactivity and alienation is death for the soul. It was for Harry. It is for us as well.

Our individual relational reality was born of the con- nection of our parents. Without the loving and nurturing presence of others after birth, we would not have survived. The relationships in our family of origin shaped and molded our lives. As we grew into adulthood, our relationships influ- enced the state of our souls for good or for ill.

We cannot reach our potential without healthy relationships. Like an acorn maturing into a mighty oak, we grow into maturity through healthy relationships. Life-giving relationships are the source and the fruit of life. When our relationships foster ap- propriate connection and lead to deep communion with others, we become more fully alive. Deep and meaningful relationships are both the means and the result of living into our potential.

Profound relational connection and communion is "the narrow way" Jesus spoke of. We may live in an incredible house and have a wonderful job, but if our closest relation- ships are fractured, life is miserable. Wealth and power prove to be poor substitutes for matters of the heart. The reason we might "gain the whole world but lose [our] own soul" (Matthew

16:26) is simple—we are constituted relationally. We are neurologically configured for and by relationships. Why do we carry this design?

DESIGNED IN THE IMAGE OF THE TRINITARIAN GOD

We are relational beings because we are created in the image of a relational God. By definition the Christian God exists in relationship as Father, Son and Spirit. While existing as three distinct persons, they share one divine essence that is described as love (1 John 4:8). God can *be* love only if God exists as community. The pure love the divine persons have for each other is unconditionally giving in its character. The Father gives himself for the Son, and the Son gives himself for the Father. The gift of each for the other is personified in the Spirit. And not only do they give unconditionally, they receive each other in the same manner. That is the nature of *agapē*. It is radical giving *and* receiving. It is perfect communion and union. It is truly beautiful and good.

We were created with this relational likeness and we long for relational connection because God exists in a relationship of love. God designed us to enjoy giving and receiving. God designed us to be *for* another. God designed us to receive *from* another. We even receive our understanding of our self in realtionship with another. This is what it means to be a relational being. Because we bear God's relational likeness, we can commune with God. We also have the capability of connecting with each other in mutually self-flourishing ways.

DESIGNED AS MALE AND FEMALE

Maleness and femaleness is the fundamental way we carry our

relational design. Interestingly, the English word *sexuality* comes from the Latin word *sexus*, which means "being divided, cut off, separated from another." We typically don't think of sexuality in terms of separation, but that is precisely what it is. Our sexual desire, drive and energy show we are separated and long to be connected (both physically and emotionally).

When Adam was alone, God said his condition was not good. So God brought the animals to Adam for the purpose of finding a partner. Since no animal could be his soulmate, God created a "suitable" companion. The Hebrew word here suggests correspondence to Adam's nature. This companion would be his "helper." The Hebrew word here carries the idea of mutual support. We can think in terms of an A-frame building—each side needs the other in order to maintain its integrity.

Needless to say, Adam was a happy man. To his delight he now had an answer to his incompleteness. He was no longer alone and separated. He could now communicate, connect and commune with one who was like him. God pronounced this state of affairs "good."

Even though Adam could commune with his Creator, "it is not good for the man to be alone" (Genesis 2:18). God knew Adam needed communion and union with another human. Out of love Adam and Eve were created as distinct individuals (male and female) who, like the trinitarian God, enjoyed community. Eve was Adam's exact counterpart. Their maleness and femaleness became mutually life giving in many ways.

Why do we feel so much energy in our sexuality? Because we are created by and for intimacy. Our sexual energy is proof of our relational essence. We can hardly stand a "divided" condition because we are relational at our core. We will feel most alive in healthy relationships (including but not limited to marriage). We feel most dead or separated in unhealthy relationships (or no relationship).

Harry found this to be true. He had lost his most significant relational connections. And when he lost them he lost what God had etched into the very fabric of his being. Relationships are not just important priorities. They are essential for our physical, psychological, emotional and spiritual well-being. We cannot live fully alive apart from loving connection with others. Even God is constituted this way.

OUR RELATIONAL UNIVERSE

We are structured by and for relationships. Our relationships determine whether we have and enjoy life. A deep participation in the life of another is the lifeblood of the soul. Relational connection is *that* profound and *that* necessary. It is *that* basic.

But the necessity of relational participation is not only a human reality. The relational reality implanted in our DNA is also at the core of the universe. *All reality is relational.* That is to say, all of creation is designed *for* someone or something else, and all of creation is designed to receive *from* someone or something. A flourishing universe depends on the relational design of HEALTHY giving and receiving.

From a Christian perspective the universe receives the gift of life from God, who is present in all of the created order. God actually participates in the world, and the world finds its life in God. God didn't merely create the world: God sustains the world; God inhabits the world. Without the Spirit of God giving life to the created order it would cease to exist. There is no place where we can escape God's presence (Psalm

139:7-8). God has a life-giving relationship with the universe, and the universe has a life-dependent relationship with God. As Scripture says, "When you send your Spirit, new life is born to replenish all the living of the earth" (Psalm 104:30).

This is what Paul affirmed when he said to the Athenians, "For in him we live and move and exist" (Acts 17:28). He made it clear that God "gives life and breath to everything, and he satisfies every need" (Acts 17:25). Paul is more explicit and specific in the book of Colossians. Speaking of Christ's role in sustaining life he writes, "He [Christ] existed before everything else, and he holds all creation together" (Colossians 1:17). Christ is the source of life, the cosmic nucleus around which all creation revolves. Apart from his continuous, actual relational presence, the world would cease to exist.

From Old Testament times through the first fifteen hundred years of Christianity it was assumed that God was actually present and actively enlivening all of life. People took for granted God's relational participation in all creation. It was also assumed that all creation pointed to God's sustaining presence. It was a sacramental way of seeing the world. Over the course of the last six hundred years a gradual but profound conceptual shift occurred in the West. We became secular in our orientation. In other words, from a secular perspective God no longer sustains the universe. And even if there is a God who created all (whether by immediate declaration or mediated evolution), that God is "way over there" and the world is "way over here" with a life of its own. Consequently, for most Western persons of the twenty-first century there is a radical separation between supernatural and natural realities, between the sacred and the secular.

There is a rational explanation for what we see. Natural laws govern the universe and human relationships.

To be sure, God is clearly above, beyond and distinct from his creation. He is transcendent (to use a theological term). But God is also immanent. He is close, at the center of all reality. He participates in the created order through his Son and Spirit. Even natural laws are dependent on the presence of God. A sacramental understanding honors both God's transcendence (farness) and immanence (closeness). A sacramental posture toward life says that through his Spirit God is closer to us than we are to ourselves.

We readily acknowledge the relational discontent that took place in history prior to the last six centuries. There were plenty of relational failures between individuals and nations for thousands of years. We are not idealizing the past. But a secular orientation creates another huge challenge for relationships. It displaces the mystery of God's actual life-giving presence. Gone is the vision that assumes that God's personal presence *is* the opportunity and the power to engage relationally, that God's personal presence *is* the fuel of our relational engine, that God's personal presence *is* love. Gone is the understanding that *every loving relationship we experience owes its existence to the actual presence of Christ's Spirit.* Scripture is clear that "*whatever is good and perfect comes to us from God*" (James 1:17). This includes the gift of loving, participatory, engaged relationships. So when we see children playing together, a husband lovingly engaged with his wife and friends enjoying each other's company, we are witnessing the life-giving presence of God in the created order.

We languish when God is distant, remote and uninvolved—there is ultimately little reason or capacity to trust. We are on our own, and life is too dangerous to be vulnerable. When God is "way out there" and we are "way over here," the soul suffers under the weight of its radical autonomy. It is a weight that proves too heavy to bear. Ultimately, we can wind up in narcissistic nihilism, a sense of meaningless existence where relationships are stripped of dignity. About all that is left is utility—using others for our own profit or pleasure. The radical giving and receiving that constitutes relational communion languishes. As a consequence, relationships are diminished. Is it any wonder that so often relationships today are self-serving, leaving many feeling manipulated or abused?

BRINGING IT HOME TO OUR HEARTS

Remember Harry? He lived his life in the sadness of loneliness. His relational world, like his dilapidated house, suffered greatly. His meager relational connections were superficial at best because of his unattended wounds and the feeble strategies he used against his pain. His relational brokenness, which left him anxious and afraid, drained the life from his soul. Literally.

In some way, Harry's story is everyone's story. Everyone knows the pain of loneliness at some level. And we all have our strategies for numbing it like Harry did. But often our strategies prove insufficient. If we are to love and be loved well, we will have to come to terms with both our relational design and the state of alienation we find ourselves in. If we want to relate well to others, we must honor the relational design woven into the fabric of our souls as well as the deep tear we find in it. We aren't simply frayed at the edges.

The good news is that God is at work to help us experience what we deeply desire. Soulful relationships ultimately rest on the fact that God, in Christ, has come to reclaim our relational life. Communion with God is the "narrow way" Jesus exemplified and made possible for us. The trinitarian God who lives in the eternal relationship of love is the only God who is able to reweave the fabric of the human soul. Our relational God heals our wounds, not simply by decree but by inviting us into a participatory life of communion with him.

Our Hope for You

The goal of *The Relational Soul* is to help all of us engage in relationships in more life-giving ways, to foster a journey that moves our souls from relational disconnection and loneliness to connection and communion. To that end we will investigate the impact of early relationships (both healthy and unhealthy), the attachment patterns they fostered and how the resulting learned level of intimacy plays out in relationships as adults. We will look at the challenges we all face and offer practical ways of changing how we relate.

We have coauthored this book in part because we are seeking to live what we write—that life is done best in community (even writing a book). We have very different stories that have helped us think through relational realities from different perspectives. My (Rich) dad was orphaned when he was less than a year old and was on his own at age fourteen. He married a woman from an immigrant family at a young age. They had five kids and worked hard to provide for us. They took us to church regularly but found it difficult to engage in deep relational conversation or connection with each other or with me. We lived more functionally than relationally. Even so, when my mother died when I was twenty-four it rocked my world. And consequent years as a pastor as well as some deep relational heartaches forced me to think deeply about what it takes to relate well.

My (Jim) parents served in churches and on the mission field as far back as I can remember. I had many opportunities to learn and grow in my faith. I followed in my dad's footsteps and entered full-time pastoral ministry after Bible college and seminary. From all appearances I had far more advantages than Rich did. But that simply made my relational challenges more difficult to see and acknowledge. In my late forties my mom's death touched me so deeply that I could no longer hide from my pain. The wheels came off my relational wagon.

So both of us have our baggage. We are wounded writers. It is our conviction that no one enters life ready-made for communion with God or others. Certainly neither of us did. Much of what we have learned has come by way of much relational pain. But we have tried to be honest with ourselves and with you because we are convinced that living from a deeply relational perspective (modality) is what all of us must do if we are to thrive in life. We share what we have learned from a posture of humility and gratitude.

What we have discovered in ourselves, in Scripture and in working with many people through the years is that the foundation for relational connection and communion is the capacity to trust appropriately and well. Trust enables us to be present to God and others with fewer defenses. Trust fosters the openness, attentiveness, curiosity, acceptance and forgiveness needed for healthy relationships.

A lack of trust leads to alienation. That's what happened to Adam and Eve. At the root of their disobedience was mistrust in the goodness of God. So if we are going to relate well to God and others, we need to get to the bottom of our mistrust and find out how we can change. We cannot love well or be loved well without trust. And so you will find a lot about trust in these pages.

One last word before we move forward. Healthy, rewarding relationships are the result of both grace and grit. There are things we must do to foster "true self" living (that is, the *giving* and *receiving* posture of a trusting soul that is needed for connection and communion with others). There are things we must do to relinquish "false self" living (the *taking* and *defending* posture of a mistrusting soul who starves and sabotages relationships). The questions at the end of each chapter will help you (and your small groups) apply the stories and principles to your relational soul.

But ultimately, relational connection is the gracious gift of the triune God. Deep connection is possible because God is *for* us. In eternity past the Father determined to draw us into loving communion by placing us in his Son through the Spirit. The relational reality in which we participate with God changes our identity, our capacity to trust and our relationships.

So we welcome you into this journey. *The Relational Soul* is both a map and a compass by which we can live in our receptive true-self reality rather than our reactive false-self reality. If you long for something more with God and others, we invite you to join us on this journey. It starts not by kicking down doors but by opening the door of our souls to the One who is always knocking. When we accept his invitation, we discover our life is lived in the very life of the triune God. Conscious participation in the love of the Father, Son and Spirit makes all the difference in our connection with others.

All of us need help in our relational journey. We trust that this book will prove helpful to you. We also encourage you to connect with CrossPoint ministries. More information about what we have to offer can be found at the back of the book.

FOR REFLECTION AND DISCUSSION

1. Can you identify in any way with Harry? If so, how?

2. What is the significance for you of the fact that God is a relational God?

3. In what way does gender contribute to soulful relationships?

4. What are some of the practical implications of the fact that the Spirit of God is in and empowering every relationship?

5. How have you masked your relational wounds and feelings of loneliness?

6. If you were to identify what you long for relationally, what would you say?

7. In what relationships would you like to cultivate a greater experience of closeness?

2

ATTACHMENT

Learning to Relate Starts Early in Life

Chad and Elaine had been married for eighteen years. Even though they had a lot going for them, they felt they had reached a plateau. Elaine felt their relationship was stale because they weren't spending enough time together. Chad agreed that he and Elaine weren't close, but he didn't know what they could do about it. Busy with two teenagers and a "surprise" who was beginning kindergarten, their days were full. Chad was an executive in a national firm, and Elaine's work kept her away from home many nights.

Elaine summarized things this way: "After eighteen years I thought we would be closer and in a different place emotionally. But we just have a routine with our kids and friends. We are stuck." Chad's take was that Elaine was never satisfied, always wanted something more and complained too much. Yes, he wanted to be closer, but this was about as good as things could be in light of their demanding jobs, the care of their kids and their involvement in their church and community.

Their emotional frustration led to a typical relational pattern. Elaine would reach a threshold and express the frustration of her loneliness to Chad. He would nod, say something about how he wanted more but that everyone was busy. Then he would withdraw. Eighteen years of this relational dance had turned Elaine's frustration into anger and resentment. "For years I've reached out to him. He listens, but nothing changes. He does things for everyone else but doesn't really reach out to me. I can't live like this any more." She wanted out. Chad was sad. "I try to connect more with her but don't know how. I think she's too idealistic. I love her, but she wants more than I can give."

THE EARLY AND ENDURING CONNECTION CENTER

Chad and Elaine loved God, their kids and each other as best they knew how. They were serving in their church. Neither was emotionally involved with someone outside the marriage. But for both something big was missing. It was the ability to connect deeply at an emotional level in a sustained way. The trouble was that neither knew how to change. Both sensed that their full schedule wasn't the real reason for their distance. Something deep inside seemed to keep them from what they longed for with each other. Elaine would pursue Chad out of desperation. Chad would try to respond positively but then would emotionally withdraw even when he really didn't want to do so.

What was happening? As you might guess, their early memories of life help provide the answer. Elaine's parents were good people but inconsistent in their care. Sometimes they made her feel special and other times they were very much emotionally unavailable. She had always been a good girl and tried to do whatever she could to keep the affection that seemed to come and go. Chad's parents seemed distant to him. Because of their divorce when he was very young, they were preoccupied with their own lives. He had learned to make it on his own without their emotional involvement in his life.

Learning to relate starts at least as early as the day we are born (and probably in the womb). Our way of entering into and maintaining *all* our relationships (not just marriage) is one of the earliest psychological structures formed in us. We come into the world neurologically wired to make connections, to attach to others. When our early connections are healthy, we will find it easier to connect well as adults. To the extent our emotional attachment with our primary caregivers is lacking while we are children, we will find our relational capacity limited as adults.

It is virtually impossible to overstate the significance of our learned relational attachment system in the early years and its profound influence on our relational experience as adults. *The quality and character of the programming we received early in life establishes a pattern of attachment that controls our relationships later in life.* This was the lesson Chad and Elaine began to learn.

We are able to attach to others because our souls are relational *and* permeable. God designed us to absorb the presence of others, especially when we are young. Two primitive instincts are in service of the infant's attachment design. First is the sucking instinct. It fosters a bond with the mother whereby the child absorbs both the physical and emotional needs of the young soul. Second is the instinctual search for the gaze of another's eyes. Looking for and locking on to the eyes of another also fosters a bond. These instincts build the neural network that compels the infant's connection with others.

The attachment system is so significant and comprehensive that it literally organizes and influences the development of other critical neurological systems in the body. Our feelings, will and memory come under its domain in the first months of life. When our cognition comes online later, it will also be under the influence of our attachment system. In other words, the attachment network compels us *to* connect with others, and it eventually controls *how* we connect with others.

Four Relational Patterns

In the 1970s John Bowlby pioneered the study of early attachment. Since then there has been a great deal of research that has identified four basic patterns of attaching: avoidant, ambivalent, scattered and stable. All of us learn one of these basic patterns early in life, and it becomes the way we tend to engage relationally throughout our lives. How we learn to relate in childhood will influence how we relate as an adult— unless or until the adult makes an intentional, hard-fought shift.

Before looking at each of the four patterns, we need to highlight one crucial reality. *The primary factor that determines the pattern a child will land on is trust.* Trust is born and nurtured in the infant through the consistent and reliable care of the primary caregivers. Trust is the critical, nonnegotiable element required for learning to attach well. Mistrust interrupts the growth of the healthy giving and receiving necessary for appropriate relational connection. Simply put, without the ability to trust oneself and others well, intimacy is blocked. Notice how the capacity to trust plays out in the four patterns.

Avoidant attachment pattern. When the primary care-givers are consistently *unavailable*, a child learns to avoid trusting others. The learning is not conscious, but it is profound. When mom or dad routinely fails to show up emotionally, a child experiences the pain of anxiety. Over time the child learns to defend against the pain by avoiding others emotionally. He unconsciously begins to feel it is better to be distant than disappointed.

A person with an *avoidant* pattern of engaging and connecting keeps a certain distance in even the closest of adult relationships. There is a basic and underlying distrust of others because they probably will not show up when most needed. A person does not become too dependent lest he (or she) suffer again the anxiety and frustration of others not being emotionally present. If an individual doesn't open his soul deeply to another, then he cannot be deeply hurt by another. He can only trust himself.

This is the attachment pattern Chad learned. His capacity for intimacy was inhibited because intimacy requires the capacity to trust one's heart to another. Chad wanted but struggled mightily to do so. His way of relating, which he learned early in childhood, would have to change if he was going to be deeply available to Elaine.

But something even more profound began to occur to Chad. It slowly dawned on him that his pattern of relating to Elaine was his pattern of relating to God. Yes, he was committed to God like he was committed to Elaine. He covered the functional bases of going to church and serving his family and others. But in both his relationship with Elaine *and* with God something was missing. Chad stumbled onto the principle that governs all our relationships—*how we relate is how we relate*. Or to quote the apostle John, "If we don't love people we can see, how can we love God, whom we cannot see?" (1 John 4:20).

Ambivalent attachment pattern. When the primary caregivers are consistently *unreliable*, a child learns to avoid trusting herself (or himself). When there seems to be no reason for mom's or dad's erratic emotional availability, even though they may be consistently present, the child has no other choice than to assume the changes in the parents are due to a major flaw in her soul. *Others seem to be trustworthy (at least at times), but I must not be trustworthy.* She learns to trust others but doesn't learn to trust herself.

When a child's attachment need is provoked but not satisfied deeply because the parent's presence proves unreliable, she typically becomes clingy and dependent. She doesn't want to risk losing affection and approval. The loss would only prove her to be untrustworthy. Thus she becomes externally focused, desperately looking for someone to attach to who will consistently be emotionally available.

As a person grows into adulthood there will always be an exaggerated yearning for something more from others. There is an ill-defined sense of self and thus an overdependency on others for a sense of identity. Naturally, intimacy is diminished because true intimacy requires two individual persons, not one person psychologically making up for the other's deficiency. A person has to have a basic level of trust in oneself to be able to show up for another.

This is where Elaine found herself. She was constantly longing for more emotional connection with Chad in order to feel whole as a person. And like Chad, Elaine discovered that her relational pattern with God was the same as with her husband. She talked a lot about God and was even perceived by others as highly spiritually attuned to God, but her actual experience with God was limited. It felt more like desperation than communion. Again, the principle is true—how we relate is how we relate. If we have learned to be ambivalent with others, we will be ambivalent in our relationship with God.

Scattered attachment pattern. The third pattern is what typically happens in a child when the primary caregivers are *both unavailable and unreliable*. When dad and mom are avoidant, chaotic and overly dependent on the child in capricious and inconsistent ways, the child's ability to develop trust with anyone will be severely handicapped. The child suffers the worst of both the avoidant and ambivalent attachment patterns. The child can trust no one, not even him- or herself.

The internal experience of an adult with a scattered pattern is confusing. It is a strange mixture of exaggerated, needy dependency *and* restless, confusing avoidance. The person pulls others in and then pushes them away. His or her experience of emotional closeness is sometimes intense and then quickly cool. Obviously, those with a scattered attachment pattern create substantial relational conflict and confusion in others.

The same characteristics emerge in one's relationship with God. The experience of communion with God is a troubled journey of strong feelings of dependency and then profound feelings of distance. Often the scattered soul becomes fatigued by the emotional swings and consequently finds it difficult to cultivate a consistent and stable experience of spiritual maturity.

Stable attachment pattern. The fourth pattern is what develops in a child whose caregivers are *both reliably and consistently emotionally present.* As a result, a child progressively learns to trust others and oneself. This pattern offers the best possibility for a consistent experience of intimacy in adulthood. As an adult the person is able to rely on those who are close, but is also able to stand as an individual. This pattern of attachment leads mature adults to experience intimacy with God. However, it can prove so stable that the person feels little need for God. The pride of exaggerated reliance on one's own abilities and relationships can prove to be a stumbling block to trusting God.

THE EMOTIONAL THERMOSTAT

Our attachment pattern contributes to the level of closeness that makes us feel safe. For some, closeness creates anxiety. For others, separation creates anxiety. This learned level of closeness in which we feel safe is called the "proximity principle" or our "learned level of intimacy."

The proximity principle functions much like the thermostat that regulates the temperature in a house. When the temperature drops the thermostat registers the drop and starts the furnace to bring the temperature back up to the thermostat setting. When the temperature climbs the thermostat registers the increase and starts the air conditioner to bring the temperature back down to the thermostat setting.

When it comes to the thermostat of our learned level of emotional intimacy, there are three things to keep in mind.

First, the early setting becomes our normal. No matter where our attachment pattern sets the thermostat, it becomes our emotional comfort zone. Others may experience us as too hot or too cold, too close or too distant, but for us it is comfortable and exactly where we want the temperature to stay.

Second, the setting on the soul's thermostat ranges from icy cold to boiling hot, from detached to enmeshed ways of being with others. The extremely detached person is emotionally disconnected, unavailable, avoidant, unaware, uninvolved and relationally clueless. He feels aloof and snobbish, acting like he doesn't care. He keeps others at arm's length in order to feel safe, and in doing so his emotional coolness becomes his comfortable normal. In fact, his way of attaching is to be detached! This is how Chad's avoidant attachment pattern expresses itself. That is why things were so confusing to Chad. From his perspective he was doing a pretty good job of connecting with Elaine. But his avoidant attachment pattern contributed to an emotional coolness that was infuriating to her.

At the other end of the spectrum is the enmeshed person. She is emotionally needy, overly involved and dependent, exaggerated in her care giving, protectiveness and closeness. She feels invasive, smothering, meddling, prying, intrusive or interfering. This is how Elaine's ambivalent attachment pattern expresses itself.

Both Chad and Elaine were simply living out the behaviors consistent with their pattern of attaching and learned level of emotional intimacy. For Chad the thermostat was set too low. For Elaine it was set too high. In both cases the setting felt emotionally comfortable because that is where they felt secure. The challenge for their marriage was finding an emotional closeness in which they both felt comfortable and secure. And this is true not just in marriage relationships. Laity often feel pastors to be emotionally disconnected. Co-workers can unite around a task but then be relationally distant. Even friends can find themselves detaching when they thought they would always be close. All of us run into situations where, because our thermostats are set very differently, the closeness we want proves evasive. But it's not just because of our histories. There is a another factor.

The third thing to note about the thermostat is that it is defective (as if we didn't have enough to worry about already). Mind you, God's design of the thermostat is not at fault. We were created for relational connection. The hardware is good. But our thermostat has a software flaw that makes intimate relational connection elusive. The flaw is found in an existential mistrust that leads to exaggerated shame, fear and guilt in relationships. Our mistrust and ensuing exaggerated shame, fear and guilt are not just isolated feelings. These feelings are connected to our learned level of emotional intimacy. Depending on how close or distant we feel we need to be in order to feel safe, these feelings will activate behaviors that reinforce our learned level of emotional intimacy. They will move us (often unconsciously) into ways of doing life that keep the thermostat where it was set. These deep, primitive emotions help explain why we can want our relationships to be different and consciously think of ways to change, and yet find ourselves repeating the same old unhealthy relational patterns.

Christianity has an explanation for our mistrust and for these three exaggerated emotions in the soul. We will explore in subsequent chapters the Christian story and its answer to the relational problems we all face. But for now the point is that our mistrust is the enemy of intimacy. It corrupts our God-given design for relational connection. It makes the thermostat unreliable. So if we are to connect well, we need help outside ourselves. We cannot reset the thermostat of our souls on our own. And even if we could, the truth is that our thermostat is defective.

RECEPTIVE TRUST—REACTIVE MISTRUST

We've seen how the early development of Chad and Elaine set them up for challenges in their marriage. But as we noted earlier, how we relate is how we relate. You don't have to be in a marriage relationship to discover how your relational pattern shows itself. *Every* relational connection, even our relationship with God, flows out of our learned level of comfortable closeness. And as we said, the capacity to be appropriately close in relationships flows out of our capacity to trust others and ourselves well.

Trust fosters an open, receptive soul that is able to give oneself and receive the presence of another in a free, responsible and loving way. Mistrust leads to a closed, reactive soul that is unavailable to another in *both* detached *and* enmeshed ways. A receptive way of relating is the result of early relational connections in which a child felt safe, secure and deeply loved. It is marked by a willingness to be present to others as they are without exaggerated evaluation, judgment or protection. The receptive person does not agree with everything others do, because suspending all judgment is clearly unwise. But the receptive person has an empathetic curiosity by which he or she engages and explores relationships without feeling overly ashamed, anxious or guilty.

By contrast, a reactive way of relating is overly anxious, fearful, suspicious, sad or angry. It is the result of early relational connections in which the child felt ignored, dismissed, rejected and inferior. Reactivity is the energy underneath the fight, flight or freeze reactions in relationships. Sometimes we fight by clanging another with denigrating and dismissive verbal assaults. Sometimes we fight by clinging to another with unrealistic and overly dependent demands. Sometimes we literally walk away, refusing to relationally engage when conflicts arise. And sometimes we don't walk away but are frozen, emotionally shut down, and give the silent treatment to others.

Reactivity ultimately owes its existence to mistrust. To the extent a child's caregivers did not provide the nurture needed for trust to flourish, the learned attachment pattern set the relational thermostat too hot (enmeshed) or too cold (detached).

It is helpful to think in terms of a continuum when it comes to the matter of trust and mistrust. Most of us fit somewhere between the two ends: receptivity and reactivity. And there are relational situations that cause us to move one direction or the other at particular times. These are not either-or categories. *But* we do have a propensity toward one side of the scale or the other. Our early history does indeed shape the soul to be fundamentally open or closed to relational engagement. We all have our particular setting in light of what we have lived (as well as our DNA, which we will get to later).

Remember the first thing we said about the emotional thermostat—its early setting becomes our normal. This means that even the most hurtful, destructive reactive way of relating is our normal way of being connected (no matter how dysfunctional it is). Don't misunderstand us. We are not saying such behavior is excusable. Nor are we minimizing the self-centeredness at the core of this kind of relating. People are responsible for their behavior and can change. We are simply saying a reactionary posture starts in childhood and governs how people learn to relate.

Unless the reactive posture is understood as a strategy in service of maintaining emotional safety through either a detached or enmeshed style of relating, we will remain trapped. If the thermostat of our learned level of intimacy is too cold *or* too hot, a healthy level of intimacy will prove elusive. The avoidant as well as ambivalent (and certainly scattered) attachment pattern makes relational connection difficult.

TAKING A LONG LOOK

Our attachment pattern and learned level of intimacy shows up most dramatically in our closest relationships. We can meet a stranger on the sidewalk and be courteous and kind. But work in business with someone, serve in ministry with someone, live in a marriage with someone and our "stuff" begins to show. When it does, we can make commitments to connect better, to be more kind, to spend more time with each other, to not let another hit our emotional buttons (the list goes on and on). But more often than not we can find ourselves back in the old, unfulfilling ways of relating. This occurs because of what is at the core of how we relate, because of our incapacity to trust appropriately.

Chad and Elaine are classic examples. Elaine the pursuer needed more time for emotional engagement. She needed face time with Chad to talk and process what was going on in their lives. But her exaggerated dependency resulted in demanding more and more of Chad. She was unaware of how her demands, rooted in her ambivalent attachment pattern, affected Chad. He would attempt to listen but soon checked out by working hard around the house. Chad put it this way: "If we just sit around and talk, who is going to clean the garage, change the oil in the car, mow the lawn, pay the bills and volunteer at church?" To be sure, someone needed to do all these things. But the tasks had become his way of avoiding intimacy. His avoidant attachment pattern was at work. He saw himself as being responsible and following through on commitments. In actuality he was emotionally anxious and physically avoiding Elaine.

To their credit, the couple became aware of their differences and deficiencies through the help of close friends and a lot of honest prayer. Elaine grew in self-confidence and found ways to constructively communicate her needs for intimacy without an exaggerated neediness that would lead to whining and criticizing. Chad began to attend to his withdrawal addiction and learned practical ways to name and express what he was feeling with Elaine. Though their marriage isn't perfect, they no longer relate to each other with the old patterns. They are now much more receptive to each other.

BRINGING IT HOME TO OUR HEARTS

Clearly, unknown and unresolved issues from the past can sabotage what we desire most deeply—communion and connection with others and, ultimately, with God. So we cannot learn to live more fully alive in relational connection without addressing our attachment pattern and learned level of intimacy. We must find out where we are on the spectrum. We must recognize the habits that serve as our normal.

This was a very hard lesson for me (Jim) to learn. Years ago, someone in my first full-time church ministry gave me the book *Emotional Intelligence*. I thanked the sincere soul, put the book on my shelf without even scanning it, and wondered why in the world someone would give me a book with that title. As far as I was concerned, I did a pretty good job of being emotionally available to my wife, kids, friends and church family. But my normal left people confused. They knew I cared and even sacrificed for them. So why couldn't I get appropriately close to them? Years later, after a lot of soul searching because of relational breakdowns with God and others, I began to see how my normal avoidant attachment pattern and low emotional thermostat setting affected my relationships. I found it difficult to trust others deeply. Consequently, I was more distant than I needed to be. That left me lonely at a profound level. Let me make it clear: I am not blaming my parents. They did the best they could considering Mom's serious sickness and Dad's schedule when I was young. They gave me many advantages throughout my life. But I had to take ownership for my relational capacity. Thankfully, God was gracious in bringing to me the presence of someone who helped me discover, deal with and develop a different way of relating. Ten years later we would write a book together. (By the way, Rich made me take Daniel Goleman's book off my shelf and work through it with him.)

If you have an avoidant or ambivalent or scattered pattern resulting in a learned level of intimacy that is more reactive than receptive, please hear us. Your reactivity will be hard to change because that has been your way of relating for most of your life. We've all learned how to be a "me" early in life, and it's hard to see because it is habitual. It is where we feel comfortably secure no matter how painful the reactivity proves to be. The first step is seeing our normal and then recognizing that no amount of willpower alone will bring the transformation we desire.

Thankfully, we don't have to remain captive to unhealthy relational patterns. Remember, we are structured *for* relationships and *by* relationships. Our souls are relational at their core. We are designed for giving and receiving. We are neurologically structured with an attachment system in our brains and bodies that compels us to connect with others. We can learn to live more fully alive with the help of others who truly care for us. This is why we said healthy relationships are the result of both grit and grace. We have to do our part when it comes to nurturing the receptive trust necessary for relational connection. But the capacity to trust and the receptivity it fosters is ultimately a gift. It is a gift emerging out of the deep, nurturing and receptive care of God's loving presence flowing through others. We learn to love well only by being loved well!

Soulful relationships are possible. But before we discuss how our souls can grow in our relational capacity, we must look further into the reasons change is so difficult. The first is found in our soul's memory (see chap. 3); the second is found in the state of our soul's aloneness (see chap. 4).

For Reflection and Discussion

1. How would you describe the emotional climate in your family of origin? How would you describe the emotional climate of your present family system?

2. Which attachment pattern most influences your style of connecting? Why?

3. How would you describe your learned level of emotional intimacy (e.g., detached, mildly detached, balanced, mildly enmeshed or enmeshed)? What led you to this conclusion?

4. How would you describe the repeated patterns of reactivity in your closest relationships? What are those patterns of thinking, feeling and behaving that you noticed are often repeated and detrimental to *your* relationships?

5. In what ways are detached *and* enmeshed ways of relating reactive?

6. If you were to become more receptive within your relationships, what might that look like? What would you do differently?

7. What do you believe are key elements in fostering trust within relationships?

3

MEMORY

Our Relational Control Center

*A*my is a bright and attractive thirty-three-year-old who leads a Christian campus ministry. From all appearances her early childhood was good. In high school she enjoyed an all-American success story—a cheerleader, lots of friends, at the top of her class academically. In college she continued to do well. It was then that she made a decision to become a follower of Christ. Her commitment and passion eventually led her into vocational Christian ministry.

She is skilled at equipping others in discipleship and evangelism. Both students and staff regularly seek her counsel and companionship. Others enjoy her kindness and insight. All agree she is highly effective in her ministry and relationships. But the fact that she is in her mid-thirties with no prospects of marriage troubles her. She dates regularly, but nothing comes of it.

"I don't like living alone. I really want to be married, have a family and continue to do ministry. At times I am angry, and other days just sad. I think I might be depressed, but I don't want to get on medication. Why do I relate well in my work but not in my most personal relationships with guys?"

Amy determined to find the answer to her question. She had always thought of her early home life in rather idealistic terms. Her parents honored the Christian faith and attended church most Sundays. She loved her mom and younger sister. She even got along well with her younger brother! But as Amy continued to honestly review her experience, her idealism began to fade, especially when it came to her dad. "I didn't want to be around him very much. Neither did my mom."

It turned out that Amy's dad was extremely controlling and never satisfied. Apparently because Amy was the oldest, he often insisted she take on tasks that felt overwhelming to her as a child. And when she finished a project, he would have something more for her to do. She often would go to her room to hide from him. At the family dinner she avoided talking with her dad. "If he noticed me, he would give me something to do. And what made it so hard is that he was never pleased with what I did. He would critique me and tell me to change something and then give me another task."

Amy recalled numerous times when her father told her she would have to stay home on Friday or Saturday nights because he wanted her to work with him. But when the time came, he would often leave without telling anyone where he was going. "If I tried to say something, he would interrupt or correct me. And if I really pressed him he would flip from being dominant and condescending to acting helpless and pathetic. It was maddening. Even Mom seemed resigned to Dad's mood swings and just did whatever she could to avoid conflict."

Once, while sharing with us some of her early memories of her father, Amy rather unexpectedly said, "I just don't trust any men." At that point there was silence. Then tears.

DIGGING INTO THE MINE OF MEMORY

Tucked away in the deep terrain of Amy's soul, buried under idealized images of her family, was a way of relating to men anchored in mistrust and avoidance. It wasn't long before the awareness of her mistrust of men gave Amy insight into her dating relationships. Inevitably she would find a reason why the man interested in her was unreliable and only wanted to use her. Even though Amy wanted to grow close to a man, she sabotaged the relationship. Her learned pattern of attaching with her father as a child was at work in her as an adult.

Though the details are different, the pattern of Amy's story is quite common. Many of us are frustrated and confused with our relational capacity and competence. In spite of what we want, the same old feelings, thoughts and behaviors repeat themselves. We feel trapped and discouraged, wondering if real relational change is possible for us.

Relating well depends on a lot more than simply making a decision to do so. It takes more than willpower or desire to transform our capacity for receptive trust (which is at the heart of all healthy relationships). The terrain of the soul is deep and complex. It is hard to access our relational control center. It's like mining for gold with a pick and shovel in the deepest part of a mine. We are looking for our attachment pattern and learned level of intimacy buried far below the surface of our conscious thinking.

So we must dig! And the mine in which we must dig is our memory. Memory is where our attachment pattern and learned level of intimacy reside. In a very real sense our memory is what makes relationships possible. Buried in the mine of memory we find how we learned to relate.

MEMORY: CONSCIOUS AND UNCONSCIOUS

Memory is a very complex and sophisticated human capacity. Much of memory is a mystery. But we do know this about it—memory operates at two levels. The first level is *conscious*. We are aware we are remembering. For example, if asked to remember something that happened to you in the sixth grade, you would consciously dig into the mine of your memory and come up with some incident. For me (Jim) sixth grade was pretty good. We had just moved from the family farm in Tennessee to northern Canada, where Dad served both white and Native Americans as a missionary. While I missed my friends in the South, the fishing and canoeing in the northern woods was so much fun that I made the transition fairly well. And on top of all the fun, I was voted the sixth-grade class president of Pinewood Elementary (even though at the time I didn't know the national anthem, "O Canada").

Memories are conscious if we are aware that we are trying to remember them and indeed do remember them. Conscious memory is sometimes called "explicit" memory. It typically comes online at around age two to three.

The second level on which memory operates is *unconscious*. We are *unaware* of what we are remembering or even that we are remembering. An easy example of unconscious memory is what happens when we ride a bicycle. Once we have learned how to ride, we do it unconsciously, without thinking about how to ride. We don't dig into the mine of memory in order to stay on the bike.

Unconscious memory is sometimes called "implicit" memory.[1] The brain systems responsible for implicit memory are online at the time of birth and are fully developed by fifteen months. Because implicit memory is active so early, what is remembered are not episodes recorded in words or pictures. Instead, this memory is recorded in emotions, perceptions, bodily sensations and the body's readiness to respond in certain ways. Back to the bicycle example—though we can describe it verbally, we don't remember riding a bike in words. We remember in and with our body. This is the way God designed us as embodied souls.

While there are many fascinating aspects to implicit memory, two are critical when it comes to our relationships. First, we usually are not consciously aware of what is being encoded in this memory. In other words, we don't have to pay attention for something to be absorbed in our implicit memory. Second, we are not aware that it is operating. But this doesn't mean implicit memory has little effect on us; just the opposite is the case. *Implicit memory has an enormous effect on us because it holds our way of relating.*

Implicit Memory and Relationships

Implicit memory stores our relational habits and evaluations—our way of attaching to others (attachment pattern) and how close we feel we can be to others and still feel safe (learned level of intimacy). The kind of memory that makes it possible to ride a bicycle is the same memory that makes it possible to connect with others. And this kind of memory is very difficult to put into words. It is an emotional way of knowing almost beyond words.

Implicit memory is always active in all our relationships. It shapes the way we perceive, process and present ourselves in our relational world. It guides how we respond and interact. Daniel Siegel summarizes, "relational experiences involve knowledge or information that is packaged in intuition, feelings, and gut-level sense that go on outside of our conscious awareness."[2] Because our implicit relational knowledge is stored in the unconscious part of memory, how important people in our life feel about us is remembered not "in words, but in our emotions, body, and images in our gut-level way of knowing."[3]

Online at birth, our implicit memory gets programmed early. We acquire a basic blueprint for how to build relational experiences. Our blueprint then sets us up for how we go about our relationships in ways that *reinforce our original relational experiences.* In other words, our early programming directly affects the way we perceive and process relationally so that we usually engage relationally in ways that confirm our early programming.

This was Amy's experience. She learned a way of relating to men from her domineering, intrusive, unreliable and self-centered father. Her way of relating to men was embedded in the emotions that served as her blueprint of how to relate to any man who attempted to get close to her. Amy's implicit memory was programmed to avoid emotional intimacy with men and thus she had no deep connections with them. Her way of perceiving and responding was so powerful that it sabotaged what Amy consciously wanted to happen. She was looking for someone she could love for the rest of her life. But her implicit memory made sure that didn't happen.

Amy was unaware of how her implicit memory affected her relationally. Many of us are like her. We are not consciously aware of how our present relationships find their template in what we absorbed as children. But the truth is clear—if our implicit memory is reactive, as it was for Amy, then we will relate in ways that confirm our need to be reactive. We will live out our unconscious emotional blueprint.

Implicit memory is the means by which we do relationships in ways that are unconscious to us. We typically don't recall the details of how we learned to attach. We typically don't think about how we came about our learned level of emotional intimacy. We typically don't think about how we practice our way of relating. But our implicit memory keeps what we learned alive and active in all our relationships as adults, especially with those who are closest to us.

MIMICRY AND PERMEABILITY

No child is consciously aware of what is being encoded in implicit memory or even that anything is being encoded. So how does the encoding happen? How does a child learn an attachment pattern so early and so thoroughly? The answer is a fascinating piece of our relational design. We are created with mirror neurons that make it possible to know the emotions of another person.

By means of mirror neurons an infant is able to borrow the emotions of the caregiver. A baby "literally uses the mature functions of the parent's brain to help organize and regulate his or her own functioning."[4] Humans learn an attachment pattern early because of our capacity to mimic the emotions of another. The basic outline or structure of our emotional blueprint is forged in the early months of our connecting because we borrow the emotional state of those who are nurturing us.

How does this work? Think of a mother calming her distraught infant. She instinctively knows her soothing emotions have the best chance of helping her child. This is because emotions breed similar emotions. Comfort breeds comfort. Conversely, anxiety breeds anxiety. The infant's neurological wiring attunes the infant to the emotions of the caregiver. The state of being of the caregiver shapes and forms the state of being of the one being cared for. "We pass down our brain circuitry to our children through our emotional communication."[5]

Mimicry is possible because of neurological wiring. But there is another factor that is even more mysterious: the permeability of the brain. Permeability is the quality that makes us open and vulnerable to the influence of others, especially when we are young. By God's design, infants cannot help but absorb the presence of others. Permeability is what makes our borrowing possible. We are designed by God to be influenced by others.

From our first day on earth relationships are critically important in shaping who we will become. We are designed *for* relationships. And we are also profoundly designed *by* relationships. We are not static, impenetrable beings. We are embodied souls, and our souls are permeable 24/7, especially as children. No wonder that Scripture uses the metaphor of "sons and daughters of God." The safety and significance we find in our new family of faith has a profound impact on our souls.

EMOTIONS, EMOTIONS, EMOTIONS

Earliest communication is emotional. A two-month-old does not cognitively comprehend words. But an infant "understands" an emotionally soothing, trustworthy presence. The child also "gets" an anxious presence. In other words, we don't think our blueprint into existence. We feel it into existence long before we can compose conscious thoughts. Because of permeability and mimicry, the dominant emotional presence available to a child fosters a receptive or reactive emotional blueprint.[6]

Thus, emotions play a critically important role in relational development. This is why it is so important to pay attention to our emotions. These sophisticated, information-processing frames of reference are buried in the mine of memory, telling us what we need and want in any given interpersonal encounter. They influence how we predict, interpret, respond to and control our relational experience.

Clearly, the capacity to think is vitally important in relationships. We are not dismissing the need to reflect well. The point is simply that our relational blueprints are, in the earliest stages of life, designed emotionally. By the time we are capable of cognitive verbal processing, substantial emotional memory has already developed. In fact, researchers have now demonstrated that *the nature of our emotional memory will give shape to the development of our cognitive processing!*[7] Every decision we make is an emotional one; which is to say, every decision is relational.

It is true that emotions are not as stable or controllable as we would like them to be. And we certainly cannot act out on every emotion we feel without doing great damage to ourselves and to others. But our emotions, not just our thoughts, must be faced and felt because they constitute a window into the deep terrain of the soul.

Unfortunately, some families don't know what to do with emotions. Some discourage emotional awareness with one-liners like "It's fine to talk about what we think, but it's a waste of time to talk about how we feel" or "Since feelings come and go, you really can't rely on your emotions." Other families are just the opposite. They are so emotionally volatile that the members, especially the children, become confused and reactive.

We must be mindful of emotions in order to understand and change how we relate. Not every emotion needs expression, but every emotion needs recognition. By doing this we honor all of who we are as beings created in the image of God. By doing this we begin to see how our emotions unconsciously influence the way we interact. By doing this we begin to own who we are.

Tell Your Story

One of the ways we gain access to the emotions at work in our implicit memory is to tell our story. Our story carries the emotional and existential meaning of our life experiences. That is to say, there are three ingredients to our story—the events that happened, the emotions we felt in light of the events, and the interpretation we (unconsciously) made in light of the events and emotions. It is interesting to note that we cannot remember events without an emotion. An emotion is underneath and surrounds every event. We can recall the things that happened to us in our past only because emotions have kept the event available for recall. We may not be aware of the emotions, but they are there even for the most insignificant memories. And at the center of our stories we find our relational blueprint. This is why we must explore our story if we want to uncover what is at work in our relationships.

I (Rich) remember vividly when my first daughter, Jennifer, left for college. I was excited for her but knew our family system would in some significant ways be changed forever. And within a week I felt depressed. Six months later I was still seriously sad. At that point it began to dawn on me that Jennifer's leaving had triggered a deeper loss, one I had suffered twenty years earlier. It was the loss of my mother when I was twenty-four years old. Since her death I had been busy finishing seminary, planting a church and trying to figure out how to be a competent pastor. It left little time for grieving, and consequently I had ignored significant parts of what I had lived. With Jennifer away at college it became very clear that my grieving over my mother's long, ugly and losing battle with cancer was unfinished. In fact, I saw that I had hardly grieved her loss at all. If I was going to escape my depression I would have to attend to how Mom's death changed our family structure, how her death left a deep void in my soul, how her death now, twenty years later, forced me to face my own mortality in a profound way. It was a difficult journey but one that reconnected me to my story and soul.

Too often some of us dismiss our personal history with thoughts like *That was then* or *It's time to grow up* or *What good will it do to remember all that old stuff?* We strongly disagree. Remembering and telling our story takes us home to ourselves. There is no possibility of soulful relationships without an integrated soul that has embraced its story (the good, the bad, the ugly).

To be sure, remembering our story is not always easy. Some stories are filled with sadness, anger, disgust, anxiety, guilt, fear and shame. To revisit them is very painful. Other stories have major gaps. To revisit them is almost impossible because there are few memories from early years. But this is the work we must do even if the memories are difficult or not forthcoming. If we long for more soulful relationships, if we truly desire to be more fully present to our spouse, our children, our friends and even to God, then we must be more present to our story. Ignoring our story conscripts us into the service of our earliest emotional blueprints and the defenses we forged in order to feel safe. Exaggerated defenses force us to live in the shallow end of the relational pool. Remembering our story, entering our story, probing our story is the way by which we own and integrate ourselves.

So we recommend that you make every effort to remember and share your story. What did you live? Who were the important people in your childhood? How did they influence you? What are your best memories? What are your most painful memories? How have your painful memories influenced your way of connecting? Answering these kinds of questions helps bring your emotional blueprint into focus.

Whenever we begin a journey down memory lane, we shouldn't be discouraged if the details are slow in coming. We can be confused or perplexed by what we remember. We can be befuddled with our feelings or lack of them. Or we can feel overwhelmed by what we lived. No matter what our experience, it is important to keep in mind one crucial thing when it comes to our stories: it isn't enough to review them on our own. We must share them with another. We must do so because we are relational beings who are both hurt *and* healed by our relationships. We must have the presence of others to help us see ourselves well. We need help even with our own story!

The act of telling our story to someone who listens well is one of the ways by which our relational blueprint becomes more endurable and available to us. In sharing our story our implicit memory is recalibrated and changed. An empathic listener helps us access and expand our understanding of our emotions and thus our conscious identity. The relationship with the listener becomes a new way of connecting and understanding old patterns. The listener gives us a healthy emotional response that we will unconsciously begin to mimic.

And while we desperately need to share with another human being, we ultimately must share our story with God. Like the prodigal son in Luke 15, we must head home to our heavenly Father, who longs for our return. The more of our story we bring to God, the greater will be the depth of our communion with God. And the more we enjoy God's presence the more we will be able to enjoy the presence of others. In coming home to God we find we are coming home to our own souls.

Whatever your story is, our conviction is this—you are held by God, and God is always listening with a loving ear. God cares about your story because God cares about you. God hears and delights in your joy. God also hears the cry of your heart. Sharing your story with God does not mean painful, shameful memories will magically disappear. But God "gets" your story. He is a suffering God. And because he has suffered in the Son, our trinitarian God offers you a way to his heart through your suffering. In your pain God's sorrow holds you, comforts you and over time heals you.

BRINGING IT HOME TO OUR HEARTS

Amy learned to be Amy in her family. She learned patterns of connecting within her family that profoundly shaped her way of being in relationships. They even perpetuated a relational disconnect with men. Though she consciously wanted things to be different, her emotional blueprint toward men made sure that didn't happen. Her story demonstrates how the care in our formative years influences the way we feel, think, desire, evaluate and choose. Within implicit memory is the perceptional compass by which we will navigate relationships and experiences with others.

In our early years we learn a way to be a me. As we grow older we become set in our ways of how to be the me that we are. Because our ways of relating become habitual, it takes a lot more than simply thinking about relational challenges to overcome them. In fact, conscious effort is not the essential element in profound soul change. Too many have tried again and again only to end up with similar results.

Our way forward is through self-clarity, knowing our story and sharing our story with others and ultimately with the One who is completely trustworthy. That is what Amy learned to do. And while she is still single, the change in her is substantial. She has recognized what was happening and has experienced a great deal of healing and recalibration in her ability to connect with men and with God. It happened in part by sharing her story with friends who cared deeply for her. We will have more to say on the matter of our stories later in the book. For now, just share your story with someone who sincerely cares about you.

FOR REFLECTION AND DISCUSSION

1. Can you identify with Amy's predicament of wanting something more only to discover you are repeating the same old patterns? If so, in what relationships does your frustration show up most clearly?

2. What are the repetitive relational patterns you are living? What effect are they having on you? On others?

3. What emotions were predominant in your family of origin? In what way did your internalize them?

4. What is the significance for you of the fact that the nature of our emotional memory gives shape to the development of our cognitive processing (that is, our emotions affect the way we think)?

5. With whom have you shared your earliest memories? What was their response? How did their response affect you?

6. What difference does it make that you are held in the loving arms of a suffering God?

7. What might be the significance of the fact that most of Scripture is in the form of story and song?

4

THE REACTIVE FALSE SELF

A Mistrusting Soul

Some years ago a pastor came to us deeply troubled. He had become preoccupied with an invitation on Craigslist to participate in illicit sex with a woman while her husband watched. After a couple weeks he responded and soon was sitting in their living room talking about their bizarre sexual request (with a handgun in his pocket in case the husband became violent). It wasn't long before he discovered they really did want to go through with what they had advertised. Fortunately, the pastor became frightened as the reality of what was about to happen dawned on him. He left before he violated his marriage vows.

A number of weeks past before he got up the nerve to tell his wife about the episode. She was devastated and insisted he get help. They wound up in our office wondering if there was any hope for him and their marriage. As his wife cried, he shook his head and slowly mumbled while staring at the floor, "How in the world did I end up in that situation. I knew it was a sin to do such a terrible thing. On top of that it was totally stupid and dangerous. I have a good wife and three beautiful girls. I would have hurt them terribly. I've repented of past sexual sins as best I know how. Why did I answer the Craigslist invitation? What is going on in me?"

Obviously, the pastor was in tall weeds. He had sinned against God, his wife and girls, his church, and himself in a profound way. He was confused and frustrated, broken and repentant over his failure. But he suspected that being deeply sorry and contrite before God and his wife would not necessarily keep him from doing something similar in the future. He was very aware that his problem was not cognitive—he knew what was right and wrong and preached it. He recognized his problem was not simply volitional—he had vowed a hundred times to avoid even looking at Craigslist. He sensed there were things "below the waterline" that were sabotaging his life.

The truth is that none of us make it through life without some major blunders. All of us have the same capacity for minor and major relational failures because we all live with a perverse power in our implicit memory. If we are to avoid relational crazy making and foster a rich communal experience with God and others, we must listen and learn what God has to say about the condition of our souls.

WHO IS SUFFICIENT FOR THESE THINGS?

God chose to create us with the capacity *for* relational connection. God also chose to develop and nurture this capacity *by* relational connection. Reflect on that for a moment. In the natural order of life we get to conceive, birth and nurture relational creatures. We participate in God's work of creating beings capable of engaging in relational connections. What an astounding privilege!

But it is also amazingly risky. On any given day there is much evidence that says God should have figured out another way to nurture relational beings. How many people do you know who trust well enough to love God with their whole heart, soul, mind and strength, and their neighbors as themselves? How many parents, mates, coworkers, parishioners and pastors do you know who have amazing relational skills? Would you sign yourself up for such a responsibility knowing what you know about yourself (the two of us would be reluctant to do that)?

The truth is that our relational capacity is, at best, disordered. Thankfully, it is not completely broken. Mothers still adore their kids. Fathers enjoy helping their kids learn to play. Couples date and marry. Friends sacrifice for each other. Soldiers give their lives for their comrades. People pray to a hearing God. The common grace of the Holy Spirit's presence in the world means we are able to engage and enjoy relationships on many different levels whether one professes faith in Christ or not.

But since the first chapters of Genesis relationships have floundered. As the account goes, Adam and Eve were connected with God and each other in profound and mutually satisfying ways. Their life-giving relationships depended on a deep trust. Confidence in the truth, goodness and beauty of God and each other made loving submission a natural and fulfilling reality. Then God's love for them came into question. The serpent said God is not good and thus not trustworthy.

As a result Adam and Eve lost faith in their Creator. They decided to do life on their own, ignoring the fact that their capacity for pure, loving relationships depended on their trust of God. (Remember, permeable souls need a loving presence to mimic if they are to become and grow in the capacity to love well.)

The consequences of their mistrust were devastating. They discovered their nakedness and clothed themselves with leaves. They hid from their Creator, who longed to commune with them in the cool of the evening. They blamed each other for their transgression. Their mistrust expressed in self-reliance and self-determination birthed shame, fear and guilt. These inhibiting emotions, once exaggerated, would disrupt and damage their ability to engage in soulful relationships with God and each other.

The emotional pain the Genesis story evokes is deep, and the implications of it are profound. God was for them, but they chose to believe God was against them. They abandoned the security of his presence for the plausible freedom of their independence. But in leaving the Garden they quickly learned that only God's presence fosters appropriate trust. They discovered that humans relate well to the extent that they are in fellowship with the One who exists in relationship as Father, Son and Spirit. You don't go from communing with God to killing your brother without something fundamentally going wrong. A joyful, content couple ended up cowering in shame, hiding in fear, blaming in guilt. Things deteriorated so profoundly that one of their sons killed his brother. And there has been a whole lot of killing since.

Our Fallen Reality

As bad as it was for Adam and Eve, the truly scary thing was that they could not pull themselves out of the mess they had made. They cast the die for themselves. They cast the die for us as well (see Romans 5:12). Experience shows that mistrust now infects our relational capacity. We are set against ourselves, others and God. We live divided, reactive lives. Not completely but certainly significantly. Like Adam and Eve, we experience the exaggerated shame, fear and guilt that flow from mistrust. But we are not just victims of our first parents but are perpetrators as well. Like them, we insist on doing life our way. Like them, we ignore the source of love and life. Like them, we mistrust the goodness of God.

The apostle Paul summarized the human condition this way: "For everyone has sinned; we all fall short of God's glorious standard" (Romans 3:23). In the New Testament sin is not merely an individual, privatized transgression of a moral standard (*sins* is typically used for specific transgressions). It is far more radical than that. *Sin is a mistrustful state of being that moves us from communion to alienation by means of disobedience and pride.*

Scripture uses the term *rebellion* to designate this state of being. Rebellion focuses on a reaction to a prescribed code of conduct. Indeed, we have all rebelled against God's holy law. The term *reactive* nuances how rebellion expresses itself in our relationships. Our reactive state of being is like a virus infecting every relationship. It is like a cancer wreaking havoc on the relational core of our very being. Because of its reactivity we fall short in our capacity for communion in profound ways. In fact, our communion experience is now restricted and ruptured. It is bruised and broken because of its reactive mistrust of God and each other. We are conscripted to our "willed aloneness."[1]

Sometimes the reactivity is dramatic and overt (for example, when a husband and wife denigrate each other with derogatory names). Sometimes it is stealthy and covert (such as when a friend or coworker emotionally withdraws and stubbornly refuses to address relational issues with us). But no matter what form it takes, our reactive mistrust is always with us. It infects our relationships with God and others. And in a profound way it alienates us from ourselves.

OUR FALSE SELF

The apostle Paul localizes our mistrust, with all of its reactive strategies, in our *flesh* (he uses the term over one hundred times). For him the flesh is an alien resident within us, wreaking havoc on our relational world (see Romans 7:16-17, 20 for the struggle it caused Paul). It is a toxin, corrupting our deepest connections with its self-absorbed, exaggeratedly self-reliant spirit.[2] It is a deep mistrust of the true, good and beautiful triune God.

Instead of the word *flesh*, we use *false self* to designate Paul's alien resident of mistrust. We are doing this for a couple reasons. Typically, when Christians think of the word *flesh* we often get preoccupied with moral evaluations and fail to recognize the psychological addictions that fuel our sin. *False self* helps point to the psychological implications of sin that are often ignored. And it also helps us keep in mind that the state of mistrust is not what God created us to be in. It truly is *false*. So we are using *false self* like others have done.[3]

In his book *The Gift of Being Yourself*, David Benner makes two observations concerning the false self. First, the false self is an image we create. Most of us create an image that is socially appropriate. As a result we receive affirmation and praise. Yet at its core, our construct is still an image, a façade. It is foreign to our truest identity as beings created in the image of God.

Second, the false self will control us if we don't own it. It's impossible to change what is false if we don't take responsibility for it. *But* it's really hard to recognize something is false when we have spent our entire life creating it. Over the course of years it becomes our "me," the image we want others to see.

On both accounts we are in the fight of our life. We are masters at creating an image. In our desperation each of us forms psychological defenses to protect ourselves from exaggerated shame, fear and guilt. We do this to feel safe and secure, because we are alone and no longer trust God completely. Some of our defenses are obvious, like walls as high and thick as any medieval fortress. Some are stealth, buried beneath the surface like land mines ready to blow if activated.

I (Jim) resonate deeply with the image making of my false self. One reason is that because my dad was a pastor and then a missionary, we had to look the part. (I felt a heavy burden for this as the oldest child.) Another reason is that I went to a very conservative religious college where a lot of evaluations were made in terms of the length of hair on the guys and the length of skirts on the girls (they could not wear slacks). One more reason is that my personality wants to look competent (even if I'm not). My false self seized on these (and many other) factors and went to work creating a "distinctively

Christian" image to protect myself from the fear of what others might think of me. And my false self held on to its created image with great tenacity. No wonder others regularly found it hard to relate to me as a person and pastor. When they tried, they were met more often than not by my image rather than something solid. And the biggest problem was that I thought my image was really me!

We are masters at creating an image, but we are novices at recognizing and repenting of the image we have created. Thus we are caught in patterns of mistrust with God and others. And when our identity is enmeshed in our image, the soul is in danger of even greater self-absorption and self-reliance. Our situation is far more desperate than dealing with a few sins. Our state of being spawns deceitful and desperate strategies that corrupt our relationships in ways we find it hard to even recognize.

Our false self influences the manner in which we feel, think, desire, choose and behave. Over time, the way we exercise these five capacities is neurologically structured within our brain. Our way of being a "me" becomes an elaborate and sophisticated way of preserving our sense of security and uniqueness. This pervasive, hidden and tenacious state of being infects our implicit memory.

This is not to say there are no aspects of goodness in the human soul. There are. No person has lost all of what it means to be created in the image of God. The false self cannot obliterate our relational design. We might think of the false self as a toxin in the water of our human capacities. Even though we can't drink polluted water, it is still water. The reactive mistrust residing in the false self has alienated us from God and gravely impacted our relational ability with others. But that doesn't mean we have no relational capability.

As we noted in chapter three, our way of being in relationships is anchored far more deeply than in our conscious choices. If making changes were simply a matter of deciding to do things differently, rewarding relationships would be easy. But they aren't. Our way of doing relationships is anchored in our relational history, and in particular our family of origin. Many of the false-self patterns forming and influencing our relational choices are generational. Many patterns are supported by our religious heritage. (The false self doesn't care what horse it rides, even a religious one, as long as it has the reins.) If we are unaware of what is going on in our souls, we will continue our patterns of relating. However, recognizing the particulars of our false-self way of being is *very* difficult. This is why changing the way we relate is so difficult. It is why we repeat the same old dysfunctional attitudes and behaviors in our relationships. It is why married couples fight over the same old stuff month after month. It is why church staff members can't get along. It is why family members feud over an inheritance.

It is also why a pastor found himself answering a bizarre Craigslist invitation. Here is what we mean: In an odd and radically distorted way his normal experience for feeling safe was anchored in his early feelings of shame. All the adults in his life routinely shamed him and, as a consequence, shame became his emotional home. Crazy as it was, he learned to feel safe in his shame. Years later as an adult he acted out in ways that perpetuated his sense of normal. He did something amazingly shameful.

All of us follow the script we learned as kids. Whatever was emotionally normal early is perpetuated in our relationships. We do whatever it takes to promote an internal sense of security, even if it is destructive to our own souls. Sometimes our actions are bizarre and glaringly crazy. Most of the time they are socially appropriate and religiously acceptable. But exaggerated shame, fear and guilt are just beneath the surface.

Whatever our strategy, our false self leaves us alienated from our deepest reality. For some the estrangement is so thorough that they have little notion of what life could really be. They settle for false intimacy in the form of pornography, romance novels or emotionally flirtatious encounters. Thankfully, most of us have a residual notion that something else is possible, that we are more than this, that what we are living isn't who we long to be. This is why the feeling of alienation is so pronounced. We can imagine a more true, more free, more real me. And we are right. Even though the false self is very persistent and pervasive, we are more than our false self.

In no way does the complexity and gravity of our situation absolve us of responsibility. To blame our reactivity on the devil or on our parents or on anyone or anything else is to doom ourselves to relational failure with God and others. If we want to change, we must own our reality before God. We must show up to God and others with a willingness to acknowledge that our false self is ubiquitous, that it is always present and at work in what we do and say. We must admit that we are living essentially in and from a false-self image. In short, we must surrender ourselves, trusting that God is good and wants to do something for us that we cannot do on our own.

Bringing It Home to Our Hearts

At the root of estrangement from God or anyone else is reactive mistrust. Toward God our mistrust demonstrates itself in thinking we can live well apart from fellowship with him and obedience to his revealed will for our lives. We are estranged from others because we cannot shake our exaggerated self-reliance and self-preoccupation. Our relational detachment is sad. We were created for communion and union. But our experience doesn't match what we long to experience. In the end estrangement is the essential and devastating consequence of the mistrusting false self. Reactivity always leads to relational breakdowns.

Merely naming something as sin or an idol is inadequate to deal with the complexity of relational dynamics. Brokenness and alienation are not addressed with a repentance that depends on willpower alone to overcome relational problems. We must come to grips with what has gone wrong at the core of our being. We must know what is happening in our souls. As John Calvin wrote years ago, "Nearly all the wisdom we possess . . . consists of two parts: the knowledge of God and of ourselves."[4]

Unfortunately, the pastor was unaware of how deeply his false self had infected his soul. He didn't see how his shame, exaggerated because of his family's belittlement, made his aloneness so acute that he put himself and his family at risk. As a result he couldn't own it. And what he couldn't own definitely controlled him even though he had repented numerous times.

Fortunately, after months of deep soul work he began to own his story. He saw how the history of constant shaming in his family led him to believe he was truly worthless. He saw how his deep-seated conviction that he was profoundly defective and would never measure up to either his father's or his grandfather's expectations unconsciously drove him to live out the script in his implicit memory. He saw how his experience of shame became so strong and powerful that it overwhelmed every ounce of his conscious moral sensibilities. He saw how he was (unconsciously) determined to prove he was his father's son! He saw how something inside him was determined to prove to himself, to his wife and kids, to his father and grandfather, to his friends and congregation that he was indeed defective, that he was shameful, that he was who he had learned to be.

Inevitably, our best attempts at false-self living come up against the harsh reality of our brokenness. When we are preoccupied with maintaining an image that the soul was not created to maintain, we grow emotionally weary. We become disillusioned and discouraged without knowing why. God feels distant and so do others. The closeness we desperately need and want eludes us. The weight of creating our own false-self identity overburdens our souls. We become susceptible to despair and bad behavior.

By God's grace the demand of making me a "me" becomes too heavy for us. We "come to our senses" like the prodigal in Luke 15. Unfortunately, it often happens after we awake up in a "far country." But, thankfully, this can be the first step to a new way of life. It proved to be for the pastor. He took ownership of his way of being and faced his false self head on, humbly acknowledging his desperate condition.

Growing our capacity for receptive trust of God, others and

ourselves requires tender humility and tough honesty. Mistrust never leads to life. We must face our soul directly and soberly. Cultivating soulful relationships is not for the faint of heart. But it can and must be done. The good news is that God makes change possible. That is the topic of chapter five.

FOR REFLECTION AND DISCUSSION

1. Why does a lack of confident trust in God lead to exaggerated shame, fear and guilt?

2. Which of the three emotions—shame, fear and guilt—do you believe is most at work in your implicit world?

3. How does thinking of sin as a state of reactive mistrust change the way you look at yourself? At others?

4. Can you name and describe the false-self patterns of your family of origin? If so, what are they? Can you identify how these patterns reach back several generations?

5. What are some of the primary ways your false self expresses itself in the ways you feel, think, desire, choose and behave?

6. What aspect of your false self is God is inviting you to surrender at this point in your life? What would surrender actually be like for you?

7. How does the story of the prodigal in Luke 15 encourage you to come to the Father?

5

GIFT OF GRACE

God's Particular Presence

*M*ac and Susan were successful by any standard. They loved each other, enjoyed two beautiful children and had succeeded beyond their wildest financial dreams. Mac had launched an online company and recently sold his share of the business for eighteen million dollars. Susan commanded respect as a competent and successful real estate broker. Though business kept them very busy, Mac and Susan honored their Christian heritage. They were members of a large church, attended regularly with their children and were financially generous. Those who knew them considered them a model Christian family.

They also made an unusual commitment to their physical health. Both worked out at a health club at least four times a week. Both had a personal trainer. Both were very conscious of their diet. Both got annual physicals to make sure all was well. It was on one of these visits that Susan's mammogram revealed a spot. She was taken aback but felt confident all would be well because of her health habits. The biopsy proved otherwise. She had aggressive breast cancer and needed immediate surgery.

Susan's cancer shook their world. But with the same determination that moved them to the top financially, they set out to beat it. Susan fought hard through many types of treatments, doing everything she was asked with a positive spirit. But after three years Susan's body, once strong and fit, finally succumbed to the ravages of her illness. She died at forty-one years, leaving Mac and her two teenage children to live life without her.

Mac's grief was overwhelming. He had lost the love of his life and felt as if his heart had been torn from his chest. They had succeeded at so much and had high expectations for the second half of life together. Now all their dreams were gone. As Mac processed his grief over the course of many weeks, one theme consistently came to the surface. He summarized it this way: "I have come to realize that though Susan and I loved each other, we were usually preoccupied with other things. I don't know if either of us really knew how to be fully present to the other in the first years of our marriage. There were times when I felt like we had a real connection of heart, but looking back those times weren't as often as I now wanted them to be."

Mac and Susan had a good marriage. They had been affectionate toward each other. They had regular date nights. Yet as the end drew near they discovered something more. Here is how he put it: "In the last months we connected much more deeply. Sometimes we didn't say much, but we were together. We were completely present to each other. I only wish I would have understood this before she got sick."

To his credit Mac grieved well and over time he experienced a shift in his thinking in light of Susan's death. One day he said, "Something deep within me is beginning to open to my children and to God like never before. I'm not sure what is going on but I feel much more attuned to the souls of others, like I was to Susan in her last months. I just feel closer to people." Mac's painful journey opened his heart in a profound way. Through his sufferings he became more available, more receptive. He learned how to participate in the pains and pleasures of life more fully. He had more room, more space for the presence of others.

A PARTICULAR PRESENCE

Because of our relational design we cannot change without the presence of others. Changing the way we learned to attach, resetting the thermostat of our learned level of intimacy and recalibrating our implicit emotional memory is ultimately beyond our ability. We can modify some aspects of our capacity, but satisfying relationships require a transformation we cannot make through self-help methods. We must have the presence of others (remember, we are created for and *by* relationships).

A transforming presence must be personal. Mimicking what we watch on TV or what we read in a book does not do the trick. We can identify and find inspiration from heroes, but we need the *actual* presence of another to experience a fundamental shift in our relational capacity. A transforming relationship is not generic or virtual; it is concrete and particular. There is a shift in our relational capacity when *a particular person shows up in particular way* in our life.

Most of us have experienced an internal change by the loving, trusting presence of another. Friends, parents, pastors, teachers, coaches, mates and colleagues have had a positive influence on us. And at the most profound level of our souls this is precisely what happens to us in and through the person of Christ. God knew our desperate need for a perfectly loving presence that could restore our capacity to love him with all our heart, soul, mind and strength. So in eternity past God determined to send his eternally begotten Son, who would bear the particular presence of the Father's love for all the world to see. And when he ascended back to heaven his presence took up residence in our embodied souls through the Spirit.

This is astounding news! In Christ God's loving presence becomes ours. So concrete was God's love in Jesus that John the apostle could write, "We saw him with our own eyes and touched him with our own hands" (1 John 1:1). John's experience of God's love did not come through an abstract idea but in a particular person. It is the particularity of God's loving presence in Christ through the Spirit that makes spiritual and relational transformation possible.

Fundamentally and ultimately our souls are restructured through the indwelling presence of the One who lives in perfect loving communion with the Father. His presence in us perfectly loves God and neighbor. His presence breaks the death grip of our false self. His presence invites us to trust deeply. His presence frees us from the alienation coming from our state of sin.

By God's design the presence of Christ often comes to us through the life of others. In Mac's case the particular presence of Christ came to him through Susan. In the context of her impending death Susan met God in an unusual way. Her false self seemed to die before her body did. As a result, she showed up for Mac with a completely available, vulnerable, trusting presence. Her transformed presence made a profound difference in their relationship as a couple as well as in his relationships after her death. Her presence transformed his presence.

PARTICIPATING IN CHRIST'S PARTICULAR PRESENCE

The particular and transforming presence of Jesus in us is the good news of the gospel. He is the reason our relational capacity finds new life. The good news of Jesus is not religious doctrine; it is not an idea; it is not a set of beliefs to be embraced. The good news is the loving presence of the trinitarian God in the person of the eternal Son dwelling within us. We have life *in him*, not in our ideas about him. We receive his life when we become like little children and trust him.

Yet his life could not become ours without his death. There was no other way to deal with our false self. It had to die for us to enjoy true-self life. It is so much a part of our nature that no spiritual surgery or chemotherapy could adequately deal with its influence. Death was the only option. So Jesus died our death, and in his death our false self died (Hebrews 1:3). The sacrificial death of Christ on the cross addresses our deepest distortions and corruptions.

Thankfully, his death was not the final word. Three days later God the Father raised Jesus from the dead. Forty days later Jesus ascended back to heaven. So now, in and by his life, death, resurrection and ascension we enter the fellowship of the Trinity by faith. We are no longer aliens separated from

God, others and ourselves. Indeed, we are now children of God in the family of God. This is such a radical experience that Jesus spoke of it in terms of a new birth (John 3:6-7). God gives us this marvelous gift of a new kind of life when we trust him (Romans 6:8; Galatians 2:20; Colossians 2:12).

It is hard to get our minds and hearts around what it means to share Christ's life, to be identified with him, to participate in him. We live in a culture of radical autonomy and individualism that makes it hard to comprehend being completely identified with someone or something other than ourself. Probably the best our society can muster is to participate in the life of our favorite sports team or movie star. But that is a far cry from the very real participation we share in Christ.

The New Testament uses a variety of imagery to help us grasp our new reality. These include body (Romans 12:4-5), building (2 Corinthians 5:1), temple (1 Corinthians 9:13), clothing (Romans 13:12), citizenship and family (Ephesians 2:19). But when it comes to our participation in Christ perhaps the most powerful picture is the analogy of marriage. Paul writes, "As the Scriptures say, 'A man leaves his father and mother and is joined to his wife, and the two are united into one.' This is a great mystery, but it is an illustration of the way Christ and the church are one" (Ephesians 5:31-32). The apostle John also used the marriage analogy: "And I saw the holy city, the new Jerusalem, coming down from God out of heaven like a beautiful bride dressed for her husband"(Revelation 21:2).

The union of a husband and wife as a picture of Christ and Christians has proved to be a constant in the history of the church because there is no human relationship as profound as that of a husband and wife. In a healthy marriage couples share their hearts, minds, bodies and life with each other. They participate in each other's life in a unique way. And in a healthy marriage each partner participates in the union without sacrificing his or her own identity. Intimacy requires the fundamental difference of distinct persons. The Trinity makes that clear.

Marriage is the best analogy we have of the nature of our life in Christ. But it is only an analogy. Even the best of marriages do not embody the mystery of our participation with Christ. So the writers of the New Testament did their best in other ways to explore what it means to participate in Christ. Paul used the prepositions *in, into, with* and *through* over 170 times to explain our relationship with Christ. John's explanations were filled with emotion (for example, 1 John 5:20). He also was the one who recorded Jesus' teaching of the vine and branches. Peter, in a style that matched his blustery personality, boldly stated that we are "partakers of the divine nature" (2 Peter 1:4 ESV). Ultimately, all the descriptions fall short of the experience of actually being in Christ, of participating in his life, of being one with him. But one thing is very clear in the New Testament—our union with Christ and Christ alone makes participation in the source of love a reality (John 17:1-3, 22-23). Jesus said, "No one can come to the Father except through me" (John 14:6). The source of deep transformation is the particular presence of Christ.

The human desire for connection with God (and thus with others at the most profound level) comes to fruition in the person of Jesus. Like a child who borrows the emotional state of her mother, we borrow Jesus' relational life with the Father.

But it is more than borrowing. We actually have the life of Christ in the person of the Holy Spirit, who lives in us because of our union with Christ. Our union with Christ is the heart of Christianity. It is the heart of our reality.

EXPERIENCING CHRIST'S PRESENCE

Because of our union with Christ we now enjoy the opportunity for communion with God. Jesus spoke of this opportunity when he said, "I am the vine; you are the branches. Those who remain in me, and I in them, will produce much fruit. For apart from me you can do nothing" (John 15:5). In this parable Jesus used the term *remain* at least ten times. It points to a deep, personal communion. It is the particular and penetrating presence of one with another.

The word used elsewhere in the New Testament of this abiding communion is *fellowship* (translated from the Greek word *koinōnia*). It means to share, to participate with someone in something specific. It speaks to the profound reality of the mutual indwelling of the Father, Son and Spirit. It also characterizes the nature of our relationship with Christ. Julie Canlis summarizes fellowship this way:

> [*Koinōnia*] is at the heart of the Christian understanding of the triune God as a rich relationship not between individuals but between persons who indwell one another in a loving harmony of friendship and communion. As such, *koinōnia* is at the center of Christian theology (the study of God), anthropology (the study of ourselves), and spirituality (the Christian pattern of experience: being led by the Spirit into God's own triune communion).[1]

Koinōnia is the experience of intense relational connection. It is the presence of God and our presence interpenetrating in ways that prove fulfilling yet mysterious. As one author writes, "The great pattern of life is the ecstasy and intimacy of God, who went out of the self to the extreme point, and so dwells among us in an intimacy we can hardly imagine."[2]

The invitation to this kind of connection is the heart of the Christian story. We can have a rich, abiding fellowship with God and others because of our union with Christ so that his life is our life. But accepting God's invitation requires our death. Jesus put it this way: "unless a kernel of wheat is planted in the soil and dies, it remains alone" (John 12:24). We must die to our reacting, mistrusting false self. As we daily surrender ourselves in childlike trust to our heavenly Father, we grow in our communion with him and others. Paul learned this lesson, and because he did he could say, "I die daily" (1 Corinthians 15:31 KJV). Daily death to the flesh makes it possible to give ourselves as a "living and holy sacrifice" (Romans 12:1).

Experiencing the presence of Christ in our lives requires us to die to what is false so that we might live to what is true. As Bonhoeffer wrote, "When Jesus calls a person, he bids them to come and die."[3] It is in the concrete, particular and daily putting to death of the self-absorbed grandiosity embedded in our false self that we find a new, resurrected life. We do this by faith from the beginning of our Christian journey to the end. As the Scripture makes clear, "It is through faith that a righteous person has life" (Galatians 3:11; see Habakkuk 2:4).

As we have noted, the particular presence of God often shows up in the particular presence of a Christian who lives in a rich *koinōnia* in Christ. Harold was such a person. In my

(Rich) early forties, life was particularly hard. My circumstances were difficult and God felt remote. Then I met Harold, a man in his sixties who was about to retire. Our early conversations centered on our common history of living in upstate New York. However, it wasn't long before I sensed something different about him. He had suffered many losses but still had an indomitable spirit. Years of deep and regular communion with God enabled him to live well with his significant limitations. He had learned to die daily to his false self, and as a result was amazingly gracious and openhearted, direct and wise. And he could laugh. He was someone I wanted to be around, so we began to meet a couple times a month. With me he minored in advice and double-majored in encouragement and perspective. At his stage in life he wasn't trying to prove something. He just loved me. In Harold the presence of Jesus washed over me to such an extent that God no longer felt remote even though my circumstances remained difficult.

Bringing It Home to Our Hearts

In the death of Susan, Mac encountered the presence of Jesus in a way he had never experienced before. Early in life he had expressed faith in Christ and had been faithful in his church as an adult. He had done reasonably well in his relationships with Susan, his kids, friends and colleagues. But something happened when he and his wife approached death. The reality of his union with Christ became more real to him through the presence of Susan. His wife was dying, and he could do nothing to save her. But it was in surrendering to the loss of their future together that he discovered the true life he had.

He discovered the transforming presence of Jesus within him. The discovery was not easy or fast. But the Spirit drew Mac deep within himself. There he experienced the One who could truly nurture his soul. As Mac was present to his deepest reality, Christ became present to his soul. The loving presence of Christ did its work in Mac's heart just as Christ's Spirit had done in Susan's soul.

What about you? Perhaps you are currently suffering the loss of someone who was close. In the middle of your grief, would you be willing to trust that there is an invitation and opportunity for a deeper capacity to connect and a greater capacity for relationships?

God offers us fullness of life. He invites us to share in the joy of his love. No longer do we need to hide; no longer do we need to be beset by exaggerated shame or fear or guilt. We are now restored, living in Christ, and Christ is living in us. We are children of God who participate by faith in the very life of the trinitarian God. But experiencing his presence will require a death-like surrender. This is the trust that Jesus says is absolutely necessary if we are going to experience the fullness of true-self living.

FOR REFLECTION AND DISCUSSION

1. Can you remember the presence of someone who truly influenced your life? In what way were you formed or transformed by this person's presence? In what way was it a particular presence?

2. Why is it necessary for God's presence to be a particular presence in Jesus? What does this imply about our ability to change ourselves?

3. When you think of your life as participating in the life of God, what comes to mind? What is stirred within your soul?

4. When Paul says you have died with and have been raised with Christ, what does he mean?

5. In light of our life participating in the life of God, what is the significance of the coming of the Holy Spirit at Pentecost? Of the Spirit's indwelling in you?

6. How has coming to terms with your limits and losses enriched your relationships?

7. What does it mean for you to die to your false self? How are you doing that daily?

6

The Receptive True Self

A Trusting Soul

*D*eborah is a graduate of a prestigious northeastern university, a devoted wife and loving mother of five children. She is beautiful, gifted, charming, smart, efficient, goal oriented and fun loving. She loves God and the people that matter most in her life. But beneath her success as an adult is a very difficult story.

Deborah has no memory of parents saying, "I love you." Instead the message she heard, especially from her mother, was that she, the only daughter, was second rate to her two older brothers. She spent her entire childhood trying to demonstrate that she was truly worthy of being loved like her brothers, but it was never enough. Though she compliantly obeyed all the family rules, even while her brothers raised hell, she never experienced her parents' approval.

When her parents told her she was not college material, she set out to prove them wrong. Because of her outstanding grades in high school she was able to enroll in a major university. For the first two years she continued to excel. But in her junior year she became pregnant. Her parents' script of one who would never measure up haunted her. *Maybe they were right, after all.* But Deborah was a fighter and didn't give in to her parents' voice. Amazingly, even after marrying Robert and giving birth to a girl, she graduated with her class. Still her parents never blessed her accomplishments. Being a good teen should have been enough. But it wasn't. A university degree should have been enough. But it wasn't. She continued to live as the lesser one.

After college Deborah embraced Robert's journey into vocational ministry as a pastor. They gave themselves fully and tireless to the work of loving others and living the gospel of Christ. Ten years later, while serving in their second church, a major fight split the congregation. Within three years both churches disappeared. After years of ministry the couple was exhausted, discouraged and without an income. "We completely gave ourselves to our church, and now we have nothing to show for all our work. If this is the way things are in ministry, I don't want anything to do with it. I should have been an investment banker. I wouldn't have earned my parents' love and respect, but at least I would have had a financial parachute."

Thankfully, Deborah and her husband wound up in a church that gave her time to reflect on her life. She was very aware of her internal voice—*You are second rate and will never be anything different.* She knew where and how that voice developed. She also realized she had been tenacious in her drive for love and respect in an attempt to rewrite the script given to her by her parents. Even so, she was no longer sure of herself or God. Though confused, lonely and afraid, one thing was clear—she was done trying to be good enough for her parents or anyone else. She was not sure of the way forward, but she knew she no longer had the energy or desire to use her willpower to overcome her sense of aloneness and alienation and be worthy of love.

In a very real sense Deborah had come to the end of herself. Yet because that had been her way of living for thirty-five years, she was very unsure of what it meant to live differently. She didn't know how to trust her giftedness and God's delight with who she is in Christ. But she was determined to live differently, to live in and from her true self.

God's Design and Desire

God's design and desire for each one of us is to live freely, joyfully and intimately. His invitation is to live with a radical receptivity toward him and others. God longs for us to express our giftedness and to believe that he delights in us. God is eager for us to live beyond strategies of coping and protecting our estranged souls. He wants us to live in and from our true selves in Christ.

Our first parents enjoyed a measure of true-self living. Adam and Eve were openly receptive to God and each other without shame, fear or guilt. They were joyfully content and deeply connected in the rewarding communion of intimacy. Their invitation was to live deeply into a participatory life in God. The only challenge to God's invitation was a willingness to relinquish any aspiration of autonomy. If they did this they would increasingly grow in their capacity and experience of communion. Their true self would mature and expand into the fullness of their union with God and each other.

Instead of trusting the goodness of God, they chose to "be like God." They opted for self-defining, self-reliant mistrust rather than finding their life in self-giving participation in the life of God. As history demonstrates, their decision did not result in life-giving independence but rather in a self-absorbed reactivity and painful estrangement. Ultimately, the autonomy of the false self proved deadly because humans are constituted as relational beings.

Yet God pursued Adam and Eve. God longed for them (and us) to be restored to his original design of trusting participation in the life of the Trinity and with each other. Scripture tells the story of a loving God taking the initiative to restore our capacity for intimacy. It is the story of God overcoming our self-absorbed mistrust. This truly is good news because though we long for deep relational connections, we cannot completely deal with our underlying problem on our own. No matter how wonderful our parents or friends are, we cannot overcome our alienation from God. We are too turned in on ourselves, too mistrusting, too influenced by shame, fear and guilt to experience the intimacy we imagine.

To restore us to the status of friends and, even more astoundingly, the status of daughters and sons in his family, God had to show up as a human being. The radical reordering of our lives could not be done by mere decree. Nor could it come through a generic or mystical connection with a generic or mystical Being. Because we are designed for personal relational communion, our redemption and restoration requires a particular relationship with a particular kind of person. Jesus was amazingly specific about the particularity of our participation when he said, "Unless you eat the flesh of the

Son of Man and drink his blood, you cannot have eternal life within you" (John 6:53).

Because Jesus lived in and from his true self, without any false-self mistrust, reactivity or defensiveness toward his Father or others, true-self living will always be found *in* him. What Adam lost (de-created), the "second Adam" found (re-created). What Adam obstinately refused to do (trust), Jesus lovingly consented to do ("Let your will be done"). *We must participate in his life so that his life becomes our life.* As the apostle Paul wrote, "For me to live is Christ" (Philippians 1:21 ESV). This is the life God designed and desires for us. This is the only life that heals us of the wounds inflicted on us by others.

THE GIFT OF THE TRUE SELF

Our true self is found in Christ. It emerges in a participatory relationship with God in the Son by the Spirit. David Benner points to this reality when he writes, "We do not find our true self by seeking it. Rather, we find it by seeking God."[1] The parable of the prodigal in Luke 15 illustrates this truth. The younger son, after reaching the end of his rope, finally returned to his father from a distant place. The unconditional love of his father surprised him. He was hoping for civility and maybe compassion. What he experienced was unconditional receptivity and overwhelming celebration.

The point Jesus was making is that the Father eagerly awaits all prodigals (even older sons). He is alert, waiting and longing for us. He is lavish in his love, embracing all we are, not just some of what we are. His receptivity makes us participants in his life. His receptivity makes space for us within the divine communion of Father, Son and Spirit. In this participatory relationship we become what God designed and declared us to be, new creations in Christ (2 Corinthians 5:17 ESV).

Our truest identity is not a self we create but the self that God creates and freely gives to us in Christ. We embrace the gift as we live in a participatory experience of a particular communion with the triune God. We live into God's gift as we open our souls to his love for us in Christ. *But to open our hearts to God we must be able and willing to trust.* We have to be willing to go home to the Father. To the extent we trust the goodness of God who is *for* us, we will enjoy the gift that is ours. This is why we made such a big deal about attachment patterns and one's learned level of intimacy in chapter two. *The soul's first task is to learn to trust, because our capacity to trust is our capacity to love and be loved, to give and to receive.* The same could be said of the Christian life—it is based on cultivating and expressing a deepening trust in Christ.

So the way to true-self living is not through creative effort but through surrender to the God whose arms are open to us. True-self living is by faith. Faith is the willingness to relinquish, to trust. It is a willingness to renounce our self-reliance and to claim life as a gift. It is a gift we receive. This is what Deborah learned. As she relinquished her efforts to create a self (which is false), her true self was reborn, restored and renewed. It emerged and matured not by self-determined efforts but rather by intentionally yielding herself to her heavenly Father.

Our true self thrives in the surrender of humility and gratitude to the loving, triune God. Christ's life becomes our life and calls forth what is true, real and authentic in us. We come to know at the core of our being that apart from the presence of Christ, true-self living is impossible (not just hard). We realize we cannot create a true self any more than we create life. It is a gift, like the gift we received at our conception. We cannot earn a true self. It is discovered in Christ. It is received by faith.

THE RECEPTIVE TRUE SELF

True-self living expresses itself in receptivity toward God and others. Receptivity is the fruit of trusting God and others. It is also the fruit of trusting what is most true about ourselves, of who God has created us to be, of who we are in Christ. Jesus knew at the core of his being that his Father was gracious and receptive. His Father's love for him gave birth to his love for his Father and his ability to live into what was truly true within him. To the extent we participate by faith in the life of Jesus, we grow more receptive and less reactive. We trust who God has made us to be in Christ, and we live from that solid, anchored, true reality.

We receive others into the grace we have received and now live in. We forgive because we are forgiven. We bless because we are blessed. We love because we are loved. As we do this we bear the presence of God to others (2 Corinthians 2:14; 5:20). God's grace and truth empowers us to grow beyond our pretensions, our posturing and our protectiveness of idealized goodness. We live as wounded healers. We are open to others, able to be seen, able to be heard and able to be known. We grow in the generosity of a receptive presence.

Henri Nouwen describes the receptivity of true-self living with the word *hospitality*. He notes that the essential movement of the soul is from hostility (the reactive false self) to the radical Christlike posture of hospitality (the receptive true self). "Hospitality, therefore, means primarily the creation of a free space where the stranger can enter and become a friend instead of an enemy. Hospitality is not to change people, but to offer them space where change can take place."[2]

A receptive presence is marked by the grace of God's receptivity. Our presence will be a hospitable presence as it bears the hospitality of God that offers a welcoming space, a space of rest and comfort, a space of grace and truth. Our ultimate and essential purpose is that the wayfarer and wanderer, the successful and the broken, the accomplished and the ordinary, the person of letters and the person whose way is made by the strength of their back will encounter the love of God in our presence. It is a presence willing to give and receive. It creates the freedom for others to come with their wounds, their fears, their shame, their guilt and whatever else besets them.

This kind of receptivity is not something we create and manufacture. If we try, our pretentious efforts will eventually be exposed by the demands of those needing our love. Instead, this receptivity emerges from living in a participatory relationship of love with God. It emerges as we come to know God, love God and become more like God.

Over the course of our friendship, we (Rich and Jim) have had time to reflect together on our meager successes and our many failures over the years of our ministry. Looking back on our lives and knowing what we know about the relational reality of life, we have come to this conclusion: The greatest gift any of us can give another is a transforming, receptive presence. Programs, policies, strategy sessions, staff meetings and even sermons will be long forgotten. (I [Jim] am especially grateful for this since one of the members of my church board once half-jokingly said, "Each sermon you preach is better than the next!") What will bear fruit and be remembered no matter who we are or what we do is a presence that bears the receptive presence of Christ. In other words, the best thing we can do for anyone is to live in and from our true self.

MY TRUE SELF IS THE REAL ME

The false self cannot heal the wounds in our souls with its compensatory strategies. Deborah finally came to realize this. She had tried to prove she was "enough" by using her gifts to accomplish things. What she did was very good. But accomplishments, as admirable as they may be, cannot restore the soul. In fact, they deplete it. That is why Deborah had reached the end of her rope. So as best she could she surrendered her self-directed, self-reliant efforts at proving herself and instead began to trust who she was in Christ. But in doing that she also began to discover that the false self cannot express the uniqueness we bear. Our uniqueness as a person comes from the true self that God has created for his glory and that Christ redeems and nurtures. What is most true about us flourishes as we find our lives in his life. And as we live into who we are without using our gifts to try to prove something about ourselves, we find life far more fulfilling and fruitful.

In other words, our true self is not an essence that is interchangeable with anyone else. Living in fellowship with Christ does not result in a generic me desperate to confirm my worthiness. The gift of our individual true self rests in the distinctiveness we have as embodied souls. Union and communion with Christ leads us into the real, particular me that God longs for each of us to be. And in living who we are created to be we find life. This is what Søren Kierkegaard meant when he said, "And now by God's grace I shall become myself." We become our unique self as we, by grace, discover our true self in Christ.

Because true-self living is not generic but intensely specific it follows that it does not wipe out what we have lived. In other words, it does not erase our memories, our family history, what we have done. We will have a consciousness of who and what we were even though we now live in Christ. But true-self living is a radical reclamation by God in Christ of who we truly are underneath the toxicity that resulted in reactive alienation. This was Deborah's journey.

Some speak of renewal in Christ as if there is no history left for the soul. Such thinking ignores and disowns the deepest terrain of the soul. This is a deep violation of the meaning of our Lord's work of creation, the created dignity of each soul, God's providence and the significance of Christ's incarnation. The gift of my true self is the me God created and has redeemed in Christ. It is not some esoteric mystical me I never knew. Experiencing our true self brings us home to our real self. When we come home to our true self in Christ, we find the Father is waiting to celebrate us.

We set ourselves up for trouble if we think our redemption in Christ is a movement toward some idealized self. It isn't. Christ is at work in and on our individual ways thinking, feeling, desiring, choosing and behaving. In other words, redemption is not the shedding of personality. The real and concrete, actual me is redeemed and restored. The living God saves *me*! The specific and actual way I perceive, process and present myself in life is reclaimed and renewed in Christ. His presence lived uniquely in and through us is our true self.

As we die to our false self we live into the gift of our true self. This is what Jesus pointed us to by focusing on a seed falling into the ground. God gives new, more abundant life when the kernel of wheat dies (John 12:24). In the process of repeatedly dying to our false self (which has to happen every day) a paradoxical shift slowly takes place within us. We face our limitations and losses, and still find peace.

In facing and owning our limits and losses we move beyond our narcissistic grandiosity (however it finds expression). The true self moves us beyond our projected idealized sense of self. The pride that Adam and Eve had in their own "limitless" capacity to decide how they would live is something that has to die in us. If we wish to move beyond relationships that merely contain our projected idealizations, we must be willing to face the limits of our humanness. Dying to self fosters a healthy embrace of our limitations and paradoxically makes it possible to live more fully into our relationships.

God invites *all* of us, not just a few devout souls, to become who we truly are. God's invitation to live more fully into who we are in Christ honors the responsibilities and demands of our daily lives. It takes into account the ordinary and mundane that constitutes much if not most of what we do. True-self living is for those who face the challenges of paying a mortgage, raising children, surviving the demands of a competitive workplace, cultivating real friendships, healing their brokenness and managing the dynamics of an extended family. True-self living is for all who want to live in a unique way in the particular circumstances in which we find ourselves.

Bringing It Home to Our Hearts

The essence of true-self living is the capacity to trust, to surrender. The posture of true-self living is the spirit of receptivity, of openheartedness. The fruit of true-self living is communion and union.

Deborah has not arrived, but she is learning to relinquish her heart to God each day. In doing this she is declaring her loving trust of God. The more she trusts God, the more she learns of God's love and trust of her. Her journey of trust and receiving God's love for her is leading her to become increasingly receptive. Her true self is blossoming, not by efforts to fix herself or others, but by her willingness to surrender to God's love for her. She reports a growing ability to be more receptive to others without feeling as offended, frustrated and angry, even in the devastating disappointment of her mother and the church ministry. She is glad to be loved and as a consequence to be more loving.

The redemptive work of Christ's re-creation invites the real me to live in a renewed state of being. This formation process can only happen through a receptive, participatory, relational experience with the receptive, relational God. Participating in his life teaches me new patterns of thinking, feeling, desiring, choosing and behaving. A participatory relationship with God and God's people reclaims my desires so that I pursue what is true, good and beautiful. It reshapes my conscience within the wisdom of God's righteousness. It finds my behavior marked by an obedience that longs to sustain and enrich the gift of participating in the life of God.

The true self lives in a participatory communion in the life of the triune God. True-self living knows its deepest identity is with God in Christ. He is our place of safety and security. The true self anchored in God's presence is not an idealized self or the perfect self. The true self on this side of heaven is the authentic self, doing what it can to the best it can because it is bathed in grace. In the truth of Christ's presence we progressively become more and more receptive people.

None of us fully lives into our true self. None of us is completely certain of our identity. None of us always feels secure. We don't always do what we do from a perspective of grace. As a result none of us is fully hospitable, completely receptive. In this life the pollutant of our false self will continue to contaminate our true self. Yet our joy is that we are surrendered to what is real. We are giving ourselves to the One who is true and authentic. We are, as best we know how, relinquishing ourselves again and again to our Lord. It is in this journey of faith that our true self lives and grows.

FOR REFLECTION AND DISCUSSION

1. Have you ever reached the end of your rope like Deborah? What happened in your soul when you did?

2. What came to your mind when you read the statement "Our true self is found in Christ"? How does that reality impact your relationship with Christ?

3. Why is it critically important to always keep in mind that our true self is a gift from God?

4. What are the defenses of your false self that keep you from living more receptive to God, others and yourself? Why is a spirit of receptivity so vitally important for a full life?

5. What makes you uniquely you? How does that bring glory to your Creator?

6. What are some limits and losses that you have to accept about you and your life? How has making peace with them brought about a greater level of satisfaction?

7. At this time in your journey what might God be inviting you to surrender? How might God be inviting you to trust him at a deeper level?

INTERLUDE

Before We Move Forward

Wouldn't it be wonderful if we could will ourselves to be more openhearted, or if we could take a "trust pill" to enjoy deeper soulful relationships? But that is not how it works. It would be nice if our implicit memory (which holds our capacity to trust) could be recalibrated that easily. But it can't. Implicit memory requires a far deeper work if it is to let us love and be loved well. Part of the reason for this is that implicit memory is not immediately available to us. It is held in our unconscious world.

What does it take to bring about more soulful relationships? We must go through a process of awakening, weeping and recalibrating in order to increase our capacity to live more fully alive. In other words we must become increasingly aware of how we have related in the past, grieve over the limits and losses of how and what we have lived, and find a way to live more fully in and from our true self.

The transformation process of awakening, weeping and recalibrating must take place in three arenas of our lives—our understanding of ourselves, our relationships with others and our connection with God. In the next three chapters we will find specific things we can do when it comes to our own stories (chap. 7), the community of faith (chap. 8) and our walk with God (chap. 9). These chapters focus on what we must do in light of our personality and what we have lived, what we need in and from our community of faith, and how we can become more aware of God's transforming presence in and with us. Transformation in light of our participation in Christ and the work of the Holy Spirit requires something of us in all three areas.

7

Self-Understanding

Connecting Head and Heart

*D*avid was married and had three young children. He loved his wife, who he had met at college while preparing for full-time Christian ministry. They enjoyed each other and their children, and David loved his work in the church he served. But David was anxious and couldn't figure out why. "I can't sleep through the night. I keep having nightmares. During the day I find myself feeling scared and really alone. It's crazy. My wife is great, my kids are good kids and the church ministry is going really well. What is going on in me?"

After reflecting more on his situation David felt that facing his past might help provide the answers he sought. However, telling his story wouldn't be easy. In fact, there were parts of his past he had not told anyone, not even his wife. But he was so desperate for change that he courageously opened his soul to a trusted friend.

David was the surprise child born nine years after the last of his three older brothers. As a result he was often alone. The state of his parents' marriage made his loneliness worse. David's father was an alcoholic who, when sober, was kind and caring. "But when he drank he became violent and often hit my mother and my older brothers. I would go to my room and hide." David wept as he told his story, recounting the numerous times of his father's drunken rage and the fist fights between his brothers and his father. As a young boy David fell asleep many nights in the back of his bedroom closet. "It was the safest place I could find. You don't really know how frightened you are as a little kid until you live with a dad who acts like a maniac."

His parents divorced when he was four. David remembers it as a scary time. "But at least there were no more fights at home." David's mother eventually remarried after several years of barely surviving. "She met Randy, who owned his own auto body shop. We didn't have to worry anymore if there was money for food."

Randy had two sons from a previous marriage, and every other weekend they would visit their dad and stay at the house with David and his mother. They were ten and fourteen. "As bad as things were with my dad and older brothers, things got worse when Mom remarried and my stepbrothers came over. I liked playing with my stepbrother who was six years older than me. But then he started fondling me, and I didn't know what to do. He told me not to tell. Our sexual encounters went on until my early teens, when I finally told him I didn't want to do it anymore."

But the encounters didn't end with his stepbrothers. He had also been sexually active with his college roommate. "My roommate was really interested in me and one thing led to

another. I never initiated anything with him, but for three
years we were sexually involved." And there was more. "A few
years after I got married, my former roommate and I hooked
up for a weekend. I thought nothing would happen since I
was married. But I was mistaken. I've tried to forget about
what I did with him at college and that weekend, but I can't.
I'm scared because a year ago he wrote me to say he had told
his wife he is gay. I'm afraid he will tell my wife what the two
of us have done."

For years David hid a critical part of his life from everyone.
But his anxiety eventually overcame his fear of disclosure. Recognizing his desire for deeper intimacy with his wife, he took
the risk of coming clean with her. He acknowledged what he
had done in college. He admitted to hooking up with his
roommate one time during their marriage. He accepted full
responsibility for what he had done. He asked for forgiveness.

True-self living requires the willingness to embrace and tell
our story. All of our story. This is what David did. He opened
his heart to the presence of the one who loved him. He owned
what he had lived. Through the vulnerability of confession he
integrated his story into his identity in the presence of his
wife. There were months of significant emotional dissonance
between them. The journey wasn't easy. But to his wife's
credit she was able to work through the process of forgiveness.
And the grace of forgiveness has strengthened their marriage
and brought them into a truer place of connection.

OUR STORY IS OUR IDENTITY

Our story gives rise to our identity. When people meet
someone for the first time and try to get to know each other,

they don't say, "I'm a mixture of compulsive defenses seeking to compensate for my inability to trust at a deep level." While all those things may be true, that is not where we begin. In order to give another a glimpse into our identity we tell a bit of our story—where we were born, where we've lived, what we do and so forth.

But many people don't really know their story. Here is one reason why. Our story is composed of three things—events, emotions (surrounding the events we experienced) and interpretations (what we think we learned from the events and emotions of our lives). Events and emotions don't become a story without an interpretation. Our interpretation is the script of our lives. It becomes my identity, and I become my interpretation. For example, if I suffered a great deal of significant losses in my life (events) and felt a lot of sadness over those losses (emotion), it could be easy to decide, *I'm not going to ever get too close to anyone or anything* (interpretation). My identity would be that of an aloof person.

Our explicit and implicit memory holds our story. The events (and often emotions) are registered in explicit memory. We can recall things that happened to us. We cannot change what we explicitly remember (that is, what happened to us and what we felt about that). Thankfully, we don't have to change them. God takes all of what we have experienced and draws it into our true self.

But our story is also held in our implicit memory. Specifically, our interpretation of our life is always relational at its core, and the core of our relational wiring is in our implicit world. The events and emotions of our lives are interpreted primarily in terms of how we relate to others. This is why getting to the implicit realities of our story is foundational to soulful relationships. We have developed interpretations that affect our relationships. Without seeing what they are and why they are the way they are, we cannot move any deeper in our connections with God and others. We must get to both the conscious and unconscious realities of our story. We must do so because *whatever we do not own will eventually own us.* Our interpretation will dictate how we engage relationally.

THE STORY OF ME

We can summarize things this way—our past doesn't become our story until we connect the dots of our explicit and implicit memory. The dots of our conscious memory are the easiest to see (though we can forget or repress them). Normally, we can recall many dots of events and the emotions that flowed out of the events. It is more difficult to identify the dots of our interpretation because they are in our unconscious memory. But they can be seen, at least initially, in our peripheral vision. And slowly they can move into our direct vision.

In other words, what is held in our unconscious memory can move into our conscious memory. We can identify our interpretations. How does this happen? It would seem the answer would be a very complicated, involved, therapeutic process. But it's not. The way God designed us to see and own our interpretations of life (and thus have a clear sense of our identity) is through the telling of our story in the presence of a loving, wise person.

As we rehearse the events of our lives in the receptive presence of another, the implicit dots begin to reveal themselves. The picture of our life begins to emerge. By means of the lines drawn between the events, emotions and interpretations we see our story more clearly—the good, the bad and the ugly. As we see and own our story in the loving presence of another, our interpretations are transformed. We learn how to trust more deeply. We learn to love by being loved. This is the mystery of vulnerability, confession and repentance.

But disclosure is often difficult. It was for David. But the pain held in his implicit memory could never be addressed without the risk of sharing. He had to own his wounds and his vice. Thankfully, gracious receptivity of the embodied, lavish love of his wife provided the opportunity for David to see his life for what it really was (both the beautiful and the ugly).

Is not this the invitation of the gospel? We can own up to who we really are in the presence of God, who loves us beyond all measure. We can repent and surrender our false-self strategies to the One who lived, died, was raised and ascended to heaven. As we do, both initially and daily, the interpretation of our story changes. And when our interpretation changes so does our identity. We are children of God, co-heirs of all the Father's lavish blessings in Christ. We now can see ourselves as friends of God. We come to know truly that God is for us, holding all of our story. By the Spirit's power and presence he enables us to reinterpret our story so we can understand ourselves like he does.

God sees and knows us more fully than we can see or know ourselves. His interpretation of me leads me into a truer way of being me. His interpretation of me reinterprets my interpretation of me. What we discover from God's story is that God longs for me and I long for God. We discover our true self in Christ.

Coming to Terms with Who We Are

Our interpretation of life is relational at its core. It is held in implicit memory and influences present and future relationships in terms of how close and comfortable we can be. If we want our learned level of intimacy to increase, then our basic and primary interpretation of life must change. We cannot make peace with others without making peace with our past. For soulful relationships to flourish, something has to happen to our story.

Obviously, the events and emotions of our past are what they are. Many are good. Many are bad. But whether good or bad we cannot change them. They are what they are. I (Jim) cannot change the fact that I didn't pursue a career in aviation even though I absolutely loved airplanes as a kid and got my pilot license when I was sixteen. The only thing that can change in our story is the third factor of a story: its interpretation. The interpretation held in implicit memory must be transformed so that it is receptive to God and others. For our interpretation to shift we must come to terms with our suffering and our sin (our mistrusting state of aloneness). We must also repent of our sins (how our false self reinforces our state of aloneness through thinking and doing what is not true, good or beautiful).

Telling our story to someone who loves us is vital to the transformation process. But ultimately we need to feel the unconditional love that only the triune God gives. That love is experienced in the person of Christ. He is the hero in the greatest story of all stories. And his story has the power to reinterpret our story. It is the story of creation, de-creation, re-creation and new creation found in the Son, Scripture and the history of God's people.

As we share our story in the context of God's story there is a transformation that cultivates an openheartedness. God offers us the gift of a reinterpreted life by means of the story of Scripture. This reinterpretation opens us to true-self living, to loving receptivity. We are invited to explore and change our emotional response to early events, our interpretation and the interpretation that others provided and we borrowed as our own.

Remember the Joseph story from the book of Genesis? He was beaten, thrown into a well, hauled out of the well, sold as a slave, imprisoned in Egypt and finally freed after interpreting Pharaoh's dreams. At the end of the story there was a moving reunion with his brothers. By then Joseph had the power to destroy his brothers. But he said to them, "What you meant for evil, God intended for good." This was not minimizing life's evils with a glib one-liner. Instead it captured the words of wisdom that stand at the heart of all true-self living. They are proof that Joseph's story was reinterpreted to such an extent that he became lovingly receptive toward the family members who had betrayed him and caused such pain and loneliness.

God's word restructured Joseph's reality in a powerful way. God's voice led Joseph in the journey from revenge to restoration, from alienation to communion. This is what God is seeking to bring about in our lives. This is what God will eventually bring about in the kingdom.

Such a significant reinterpretation of life requires a deep trust in a God who is *for* us. It rests on trusting God's story. It depends on participating in the very life of Christ, who trusted the Father completely because he knew his Father was *for* him.

GOD'S SUFFERING STORY

True-self living is anchored in a participatory communion with God in Christ. The true self is open to a different interpretation of the events of our lives, including the very difficult and painful ones. It leads to soulful relationships to the extent our story is bathed and transformed by God's story.

Joseph's story was incredibly painful. So was Jesus' story. It is a story of relinquishing, suffering loss and dying. It is a story of misunderstanding, rejection and derision. It is a story of betrayal, scourging and crucifixion. This is the story we are invited to share. This is the story we are invited to participate in. This particular story brings healing to our broken lives.

Our God is a suffering God. That he is Lord of all and conquers all is only one dimension God's being. He is also the God who suffers. And he is the suffering God because he loves. Alan Lewis says, "It is God who in Christ is humbled unto death and descended to the nadir of our wretchedness and tragedy. Here God, the Judge, becomes the malefactor, judged and sentenced, and bows to the divine verdict upon human sin and guilt."[1] God is not a foreigner to suffering. He chose to enter suffering in death on the cross for our sake. In him, through the mystery of our communion in his life, our suffering bears meaning. In him and his embrace of our suffering and our death, we may come to live as our true self.

The gospel is not a self-help manual or inspiring message. It is the good news of entering into the very life of God through Christ. We are joined to God in Christ by the presence of the Holy Spirit. This life of God recalibrates all of our life and offers us an invitation to reinterpret our story in light of God's presence in and with us.

Joseph didn't come up with an idea that changed his story. His experience of God reconfigured his identity and his way of looking at the world. The reinterpreted story of Joseph flowed from his experience with God. His life was recalibrated in terms of how he saw his world (specifically, his family). His story was no longer primarily configured around the beatings and suffering he endured at the hands of greedy and envious brothers. His story was now formed by his faith in God.

Our faith is grounded in our being joined to Christ, who lived his life with God the Father. We, like Joseph, must die to our false-self interpretations. As we do, God gives us the new life of Christ. His life redeems and reinterprets our old life. By our willingness to vulnerably trust God, our story can and will be reinterpreted.

To experience true-self living we have to experience our personal Joseph journey. We must embrace our gains and especially our losses. We must be grateful, and we must grieve. We must find that God was always with us, even in the death of what we wanted most. But God gives us resurrected life. Our cross experiences still happen. Suffering continues in our world and in our lives. We are not exempt. Jesus is not the chaplain of the American dream. Our life in Christ is not a wand that magically changes what we lived; nor does it magically insulate us from pain in the future. We cannot change the events of our past any more than Christ can change the fact of his suffering. But by faith our cross experiences are reinterpreted. They are seen as a way for a new kind of life to be born.

What often continues to shape our stories (interpretations) are the implicit emotional responses to our wounds. We must be willing to attend to our wounds and address the emotions embedded in our wounds. Because our story is held by God's story, we can revisit the specifics of our wounds in light of what Jesus lived. Christ offers us a way of seeing that can transform the emotions embedded in our deepest wounds.

God's story progressively transforms the feelings that drive our implicit memories. It does so because the death of Christ ensures that God is with us in our suffering. We were not alone no matter how dark the death of losses. It is true that we may have felt and even now may feel deeply alone. Even though our present suffering may make us feel as if God is absent, he is not. God is present in our suffering. That is the promise he gives to us. He is with us because we are *in* his Son.

Suffering in and of itself is not the last word. In Christ, death gives way to resurrection. There is life. There is hope. There is beauty on the other side of suffering. In light of Christ's resurrection this conviction was the essential and pivotal reality for the apostles and the early church. Suffering occurred in their lives and many were killed, but the life within them was stronger, greater and more real than anything they suffered. As Timothy Keller says, "The biblical view of things is resurrection, not a future that is just a consolation for the life we never had, but a restoration of the life we've always wanted. This means that every horrible thing that ever happened will not only be undone and repaired but will in some way make the eventual glory and joy even greater."[2]

We have a God who is with us in our sufferings at the cross. We also have a God who is determined to bring us greater glory and joy in light of what we have suffered. We don't revel in our suffering. But in the resurrection and ascension of Christ God has promised that he will transform even our suffering into great joy. The resurrection reinterprets life. The ascension affords us a participatory life with God so that even in our suffering we are with God and God is with us. *Christ's death, resurrection, ascension and promised return radically reshapes the interpretation of our stories.*

REFLECTING ON OUR LIFE

The pain of our suffering, whether physical, relational or emotional, often crowds our consciousness. If we wish to get to implicit memory or change the suffering we hold in conscious memory, we must have space for an intentional opening to God's story. Creating space for a quiet and still openness to God with our story is not easy, but it is essential. So we must be intentional about reviewing our life. One way of doing this so we can tell our story more clearly is by means of a life map, through which we record significant events of our story, what we felt in the middle of them (and what we feel now as we review them) and the interpretations we gave our life because of what we lived and felt. (Appendix 2 offers a way to develop a life map.)

In the open space of meditation we first invite the presence of God. We intentionally remind ourselves who we are in Christ. In this quiet space with God we wait and listen. We are not trying to make something happen. We are there to surrender and be still. Our responsibility is to place ourselves before God. Often healing happens because we are willing to rest in God.

In meditation we may wish to form some mental image of being with Christ. We find a safe place with him. In this safe place we offer ourselves to him—our suffering, brokenness, failures, successes. In short, we offer all we are and all we have experienced. Then we invite the Spirit to bring events into our memory that he would like to address. Our memories may leave us feeling anxious, lonely, fearful, guilty or ashamed. These emotions are not inappropriate responses to what we lived, but they are often exaggerated in the sense that they now play a larger role in our story than is necessary or helpful. We may invite the Holy Spirit to help us discern which emotions are in play in our interpretation and whether they are exaggerated. We can reflect on our emotion in light of God's presence with us. We allow the emotion to be what it is. We offer it to God and ask him for wisdom in responding to what we are feeling. We listen for what God is saying about the emotion we are experiencing.

WHO IS LIVING MY STORY?

As important as it is to know my story, it is equally important to know who is living my story. We need to know our personality—the way we tend to perceive, process and present ourselves in our story. We must have self-clarity of who is living our particular story.

Our understanding of self-clarity is born of John Calvin's statement, "Nearly all wisdom we possess, this is to say, true and sound wisdom, consists of two parts: knowledge of God and of ourselves."[3] Self-clarity is the wisdom of knowing ourselves. We readily acknowledge there is more to our souls than we will ever comprehend. Much about the soul is a mystery. But having said that, it is imperative that we acknowledge the need for as much self-knowledge as we can.

For almost a decade we have employed the enneagram to

assist persons in understanding themselves. The enneagram suggests there are nine different personality styles, and while we have some access to all nine styles, each of us prefers to use one more than the others. Our dominant style reveals something of our personality DNA. It reveals our most primitive emotion (either shame, fear or guilt) and its level of influence on our soul. The enneagram also reveals to what extent our giftedness from God has become distorted by our false self.

The enneagram is only one instrument among many. But we have found it to be a powerful tool for self-clarity. (See appendix 3 for a brief summary of the nine personality styles and their besetting sins.) We encourage you to use as many tools as you find helpful in order to know what is happening deep within yourself. We feel strongly about this because in all our years of ministry we have never known a single person whose relationships suffered because of lack of doctrinal facts. Not one! But there are many stories of collapsed ministries, estranged marriages, distant children, failed friendships and coworker conflict because people had little self-understanding. The blindness that emerges from a lack of knowing what is going on in our souls is truly devastating.

Self-clarity is not a parlor game. It is not a self-help gig. Instead it is a journey into our hearts to see what motives are at work in our relationships. This is why self-clarity is essential for soulful relationships. From a Christian spiritual-discipline perspective self-clarity is interested in knowing and exploring the distortions and exaggerations of the soul. In other words, self-clarity helps us to face our sin and the way it plays out in our relationships.

Self-clarity is a demanding discipline for the soul to engage honestly, deeply and openly. Our false self desperately strives to manage and control our image lest we be exposed. In fact our false self prefers that we attend to peripheral matters of our self-made egoic images. This is why our spirituality can readily take on a sanctimonious superiority born of our fear to truly be known to ourselves, others and God. This is why we must see and deal with what is going on in our hearts if we are to enjoy soulful relationships.

Soulful relationships call for understanding, especially self-understanding. The self-clarity we speak of is not something we can glean and gather by ourselves. We need someone else to guide us, show us and see us. We are all afraid of this level of intimacy, but it is an indispensable passage to soulful relationships. We need a mature Christian friend, spiritual director, counselor or pastor to shepherd our own self-clarity. If we long for soulful relationships, we must take the journey of self-clarity.

Bringing It Home to Our Hearts

David could not engage his wife at the level he wanted or get past his anxiety without owning his story. His interpretation of himself had to give way to God's interpretation of him. But that required an honesty and openness with another that he had never experienced. To his credit he spoke up. To his wife's credit she embodied the story of forgiveness and radical acceptance found in Scripture. To both of their credit they are now living far more deeply in their true selves in Christ.

Our story is held in our conscious and unconscious memory, and is formed by our interpretations. True-self living invites us to understand and interpret our story in light of Jesus. Our story is held in the story of God. As we participate in the life of Christ by faith, intentionally making space to consciously experience God's presence, the deepest terrain of our soul is transformed. Changing the interpretation of our story and thus our identity is what facilitates deeper participation in our most significant relationships.

Will you take the risk of sharing yourself with another?

FOR REFLECTION AND DISCUSSION

1. Can you identify one or two critical memories that shaped your life? What are they?

2. Are there aspects of your life story you have not been able to tell? Would you be willing to do so to a trusted friend?

3. How might God's story speak directly to specific losses and points of suffering in your story?

4. What emotion is dominant in your interpretation of your life? How does it obstruct you from allowing God's grace to reinterpret your story?

5. What is your self-talk telling you about your interpretation of your story?

6. What would you like your interpretation to be?

7. Have you ever developed a life map? If not, will you begin one so that you can share your story more completely?

8

COMMUNITY

Fostering Soulful Relationships

When Rachel was four years old the Department of Family Protective Services took her out of her home. Her dad had long disappeared and her mother was a drug-abusing dancer at a local nightclub. Rachel wound up with her grandmother. After a year her grandmother became ill and Rachel was placed in her first foster home. She was in a number of homes until she was in her early teens. That's when she set out on her own.

"I was fifteen and in a relationship with a guy who was twenty-two. We lived together in the basement of his mom's home. He had various jobs, and I was a waitress. We spent most of our time trying to get drugs so we could get high."

In the three years she lived with him Rachel had one abortion. When her boyfriend became abusive, she left. "I had seen enough anger and fighting in one of the foster homes I was in. I decided I would never be in that kind of place ever again. One night when he was high he beat me harder than he had ever done before. I packed my bags, left and never went back."

Rachel went on to recount a series of difficult relationships until she was given the opportunity to work as a receptionist in a small clothing store. "I was waiting tables and the owner of the store and his wife were regular customers. They were polite, always asked how I was and always left a generous tip. Then one day they asked if I would be interested in working for them and learning to manage inventory. I jumped at the chance."

Over time Jake and Allison invited Rachel to their home for various family events. "I finally got to see a normal family. They liked each other, would play cards and board games, and talk. I loved going to their home. One afternoon Allison asked if I would like to join them at their church. I was twenty-eight and had been to church three times in my entire life. I initially said no, but then after a couple weeks I decided to go because one of their grandsons was going to be baptized. I went that Sunday and every Sunday for the next three years!"

After a few months in the church Rachel joined a community group. "The people really cared about me. They chipped in to help me buy my first car, and some of the guys in the group did minor repairs to get it running well. They taught me so much about Jesus and what he did for me. Because of them I gave myself to Christ. Now I know how to care, how to pray, how to let others love me. I've learned what it means to be loved by God and how to love others by watching them."

Rachel still works for Jake and Allison managing the store while they enjoy semi-retirement. "Jake and Allison have poured so much of themselves into me. I could never thank them enough. I have no idea where I would be without their love and desire for me to know God. I am so grateful for them. They and my church family have given me a life I could never have imagined."

Rachel discovered that the journey of true-self living unfolds in community. God used her loving community to transform her soul. It healed deep wounds and, by God's grace, forged an identity for Rachel rooted in Christ. When she said she had no idea where she would be without the community of faith, it was clear that she meant it. Her life would have remained a relational mess without the loving presence of others.

As individuals, we are never completely free of our false self on this side of heaven; neither are our communities of family and faith. So we live with realistic expectations for ourselves as well as our communities. There are times of disconnection and loneliness within our souls. And there will be mistakes and sin of imperfect love within our communities. But these experiences and seasons are held within the community of trinitarian love. *God takes the risk of fostering a receptive, open-hearted true-self way of living through the experience of flesh and blood communities.*

NURTURED BY COMMUNITY

Thomas Merton speaks plainly and honestly when he writes, "We learn to live by living together with others, and by living like them—a process which has disadvantages as well as blessings."[1] Our permeable souls have the remarkable capacity to internalize the life of others. This is God's design.

When we show up to begin our journey of life, we do so in some type of relational system. Our very life depends on it. Our family of origin, whatever its structure (for example, a two-parent home of a father and mother, a single parent home, a foster home or orphanage), provides our first community. In it we form fundamental ways of being a self. The early community gives the soul a trajectory that is incredibly powerful and remarkably enduring in both pronounced and subtle ways.

Merton has it right—we learn to live by living together with others and by living like them. We cannot recalibrate our relational capacity by reading books (although we are glad you like to learn and have chosen to read this book!) or discussing ideas. An attachment pattern that nurtures trust requires actual and personal relationships. The communities of family and faith exist for this purpose. In learning to trust our caregivers we learn to trust God, others and ourselves.

But often our family of origin is so skewed we have little chance of learning to trust. This was Rachel's experience. Neither her foster home experiences nor her relationship with her boyfriend helped her learn to trust well. They contributed to a deformation of her soul. It took a particular kind of community for her transformation into true-self living. Even if we were blessed with parents who developed well our capacity to trust, we still must learn to place our trust in the triune God. This is why God provided the community of faith. In it we learn what it means to trust as we experience the church trusting God and each other. Proclaiming and embodying the story of Scripture cultivates a trust energized by the Spirit of God.

Learning to trust others profoundly helps us all to cultivate the capacity for true and abiding, honest and open relational connections. Exaggerated inhibiting emotions such as shame, fear and guilt obstruct true relational communion. But a community of faith attends to these wounds through the gospel story preached and lived in appropriate relational experiences.

No matter what the physical or spiritual age of those within the community of faith, the significance of life together becomes vital to the very well-being of our souls. The community offers an opportunity to foster soulful relationships that nurture true-self living. Being mindful of this relational dynamic helps us understand both the responsibility and privilege of sharing life together as God's people.

By a particular kind of community. No community can be a perfect representation of the Father's love. Only Christ provides that. But still, God was at work in a particular way in the lives of particular people—Abraham, Sarah, Moses, David, Isaiah and Esther, to name a few. And these people were a part of a particular community of people, the Israelites. God's people in the Old Testament had a history of slavery and liberation, conquest and ascent to power, fall and restoration. They were not a generic group or a mythical community fashioned for the sake of telling a story. They were a real nation whose life and legacy had a redemptive purpose in the world.

God's Son, Jesus of Nazareth, appeared from within this community. Jesus Christ was not a literary creation or a religious figure fashioned by the skewed memory of disillusioned followers. Jesus was a real, historical person, as real as the community he came from. And this particular man gave birth to a community of disciples. Their life of faith gave birth to the church. All who believe in him are part of the community of faith.

God has always had a people, a community through which God draws the world to himself. If we want to understand the character and purpose of God we must look to the community of God's people. Embedded in the story of God's people is the story of God creating, saving, preserving, guiding and reclaiming. God fulfills his divine purpose in and through very real people. The church of Christ is the actual expression of his presence in the world.

The clear implication of the historicity of Israel and Jesus is this: when it comes to participation with God we can't escape the particular. Particularity is an important aspect of our true-self journey. To live in a true-self way we must live in specific, particular, concrete relationships. Because the soul is permeable and thus shaped by the internalization of others, we experience transformation by the continual internalization of the particular kind of presence found in God's people.

We are nurtured *by* relationships. In the community we learn what it means to live out the story of redemption. In the community the Spirit of God resides, encouraging, teaching and guiding its members into a deeper love for God and others. It is impossible to foster soulful relationships without a real commitment to a particular community of faith. We learn to love by loving real people. No one matures in the capacity to connect well if what we love is our idealized images of others or ourselves.

We need life together in a particular community. We are not merely living ideas; we are becoming our true self by means of the church. God's Spirit is reclaiming what was lost. Among God's people, under God's Word and through God's sacraments we are learning to surrender and thereby are maturing a child-like trust.

By a mysterious community. While the community of God's people is a particular community, it is also a community that points to something beyond itself. When Jesus confronts Saul he asks, "Why are you persecuting me?" (Acts 9:4). Clearly Jesus considers his followers to be participating in his life. The apostle Paul would later repeatedly identify the followers as the body of Christ (see 1 Corinthians 12:12-31; Ephesians 1:22-23; 3:6; 4:4; 4:12). The fact that God's Spirit lives in and among the community of faith means it is more than just a gathering of people (1 Corinthians 12:27).

The "more than" factor is a very important aspect of our life together. If we are involved in a church and become focused only on the people, we will become quite discouraged. We must attend to the "more," the mystery of God and his presence with us. The New Testament teaches that the community of faith is more than a fellowship of people with shared convictions. There is much more in the church than meets the eyes.

A healthy community finds ways to point to the mystery of God indwelling the church, as well as the mystery of who we are as the body of Christ. It points us to the miraculous mystery of the Holy Spirit, who dwells within the people of God (1 Corinthians 3:16). It teaches us how to respect mystery through the sacraments of baptism and Lord's Supper. It honors mystery in and through its liturgy.

True-self living requires particularity. It also requires

mystery. We need a community to hold these two essential realities of soulful relationships—the particular and the mysterious. Soulful relationships require both realities. The community of faith respects and honors both. But there is more.

By a messy community. Living in community, be it the community of marriage, friendships or church, is not always easy or pretty. In fact, things may get ugly. The fact that our mates are broken and frustrating discourages us. Friendships sometimes experience hard challenges and outright conflict. The strain and stress of living in a community of faith takes a toll on church members and leaders.

The challenges are real, but these are precisely what we must face in order to grow and mature in our true self. Scripture reminds us that in the midst of broken, sinful, frustrating people, God's Spirit is at work creating a transformed community. God is not surprised by our brokenness. His way of maturing us isn't thwarted. In fact, it is *in* and *by* the messiness that God does the supernatural work of drawing us into the likeness of his Son.

Grace shows up when there is brokenness and sin. The Spirit is most active when there is great work to do. Without this perspective it is hard to enter into the life of a community. And when we do not enter the community of faith we cannot increasingly live in and from our true-self reality.

DESIGNED *FOR* COMMUNITY

God designed us for relational participation. His image within us compels us toward community. True community fosters true-self living. And true-self living moves us toward community with a receptive, trusting, loving posture. Community comes first; then comes individuality. In this cycle both the community and the individual are strengthened and matured. Here are five ways community shapes our ability to live well within community.

For confronting our selfishness. We are called to community. But in any kind of community we face the intoxicating temptation of an idealized illusion. We fail to account for sin, brokenness and limitations. Community is not a fantasy league where we pick and discard players at will. As Dietrich Bonhoeffer so powerfully wrote, "He who loves his dream of community more than the Christian community itself becomes a destroyer of the latter, even though his personal intentions may be ever so honest and earnest and sacrificial."[2]

While Bonhoeffer was making reference to the church of Christ as community, we may say his words are true for any type of community, whether marriage, family or friends. Again and again persons find themselves disillusioned because of the way others are. Community exposes us. In particular, it reveals our "inward bent." To put it even more bluntly, any experience of community will, over time, make our self-centered grandiosity quite clear. In community our demand that life take shape on our terms eventually comes out. In community our insistence that others be what we need and want them to be is sooner or later exposed.

The community of faith will feel and face these temptations. We should expect this in light of the gospel story that makes much of our brokenness and sin. A realistic awareness and appraisal of our personal limitations must happen in the church. Without this we set ourselves up for unrealistic expectations that can never be fulfilled. We will demand of our human relationships what only God provides.

I (Rich) remember a time while serving as a young pastor at Peace Community Church. At the beginning of my sermon every single Sunday an elderly believer in the church tilted his head to the right and promptly closed his eyes. I was aggravated (righteously of course!) at such disrespect for the Word of God. The truth is that Louie had listened to the likes of me for more than seven decades. Nevertheless I was frustrated internally by Louie's taking a snooze at the heart of our worship time. This troubled me until I made a pastoral call to visit Louie and his wife on their farm. I had every intention of talking to Louie about his lack of respect for the preaching of Scripture. But since our time together would be my first chance of getting to know them, I decided I would begin by listening to their story.

It wasn't long before I realized the deep and painful realities they faced because of the mental illness of one of their adult sons. I had no idea of what they had gone through for many years. They lived with a capriciously angry adult son who left two elderly people living in real fear. Suddenly I thought, *Would I in my late seventies still be faithfully attending worship if there was this much pain in my soul?* I quickly gave up on the idea of confronting Louie about his "disrespect." And at the end of our visit I offered to read a psalm. Sure enough, the moment I began reading the psalm Louie titled his head to the right and closed his eyes. In that moment I realized this was how Louie quieted his soul and listened. It was his way of attending to God through his pain.

Louie's "nap" during my sermon exposed my false self. It

also exposed my uncanny ability to shroud my narcissistic grandiosity in my theology. Soon I wished that everyone would be like Louie, closing their eyes to hear God in the midst of their suffering.

This is just one small example of how community can help us live more deeply in soulful relationships. It is one of the most powerful means by which God exposes our false self and leads us graciously with one another to true-self living. As we live together in community, each of us will face our fantasies about life together. As we turn from them we can be more receptive toward others. We will then know how to show up in far more healthy ways for the community.

For surrendering and serving. A healthy community of family, faith and friends teaches us how to live a true-self life—a life of trust, receptivity and love. But learning this kind of life is no easy thing. As Gregory Jones says, it "involves the lifelong process of learning a craft."[3] True-self living is truly a craft, a way of being that is forged by God's grace working in our story and through the lives of others in the journey of faith.

When we speak of Christian living as a learned craft, we have a particular image in mind, that of an apprentice serving for years under the tutelage of a master. This is what my (Rich) grandfather did. At the age of fourteen he became an apprentice baker in Austria. Over more than a decade he learned a way of life as a baker. Finally, he became a master baker. He learned to master his craft by living with others who knew much more about it and could do it far better than he could.

This is how we learn the craft of soulful relationships. Others must teach us how to forgive, how to pray, how to give, how to be patient and how to be merciful. *Fundamentally what we must learn is how to surrender our souls in faith to the God in whose life we participate.* We must learn true-self living by living with others who are ahead of us in the journey of faith.

Learning to surrender is fundamental. All the other characteristics of the Christian life emerge from this. True surrender is not resignation or a passive giving up on life. Surrender is a Spirit-empowered act of courage. It is the willingness to offer our lives to God and trust him with the outcome. It is giving our lives to God each day, recognizing our dependency on him. It is trusting God even when what we are living is dark and confusing and something we never thought we would have to live.

When talking about surrender and service it is easy to sound idealistic. Nothing could be further from the truth. Life together, real participation with each other as family, friends or a community of faith, is ordinary, incomplete, challenging, arduous and riddled with routine. But this is the arena in which I learn to surrender myself with my grandiose notions of the way life ought to be. This is what Louie taught me in his farmhouse on a June afternoon. In his late seventies he was showing this young pastor what surrender looked like when you are an older man. He was teaching me the craft of being a follower of Jesus. At that moment we were participating in the life of God and our life together in Christ. His surrender didn't eliminate his suffering or mine, but his faith held his suffering, and that proved to be part of his surrender to God. In watching him surrender in faith I learned a way of doing the same.

Surrender, even when seemingly foolish, in time forms a quality of life that reason will never find. But this is the model we follow. Jesus surrendered himself to the Father. A healthy community does the same. In turn, we learn from the community and then, for the sake of the community, we live a life of surrendered service. And as we learn how to surrender and serve, we bring that craft back into the community in a new way. If we are unwilling to live with each other with a view toward learning and teaching the craft of the Christian life, we can expect a limited experience with God and others.

For comforting us in our suffering. My first recollection of real suffering occurred when I (Rich) was about eight and my uncle had died of leukemia. When Uncle Art finally succumbed, my parents brought me along with two of my sisters to his funeral service at a small church in Alcove, New York. My sensibilities were limited when it came to grasping the loss of someone dying in their late forties. But when my uncle's elderly father came into the church I began to get it. His head was freshly bandaged from an early morning fall on February ice. As he made his way to the front of the church he no longer could contain his grief and began to wail loudly over the death of his son.

I was startled and frightened. His open and raw grief made suffering very real. I quickly sensed suffering could overwhelm the soul. I remember how uncomfortable I was. I wanted to get out of the church building. But then something else happened. The church community came forward to where he stood at the casket. They held him, hugged him, prayed with and comforted him. Soon the silence of a funeral returned. The man who had lost his son was held by a community of faith who suffered with him. It was as if his suffering was distributed to all of us in a hundred pieces.

Our world is a place of tremendous suffering. No one has answers sufficient for our suffering. We know suffering is a part of life, and we know that suffering must be held in some way. So we hold our suffering by faith as individuals and as community. When we speak of holding our suffering, we mean a willingness to engage our suffering without becoming overcome by cynicism, sarcasm, despondency, anger and retaliation. These are strategies for coping that prove to be cul-de-sacs. They only compound our suffering.

Suffering has no answers. But it does carry an invitation. It invites us into mystery. It invites us to surrender without explanation to something we cannot understand. In the dark helplessness of our suffering something happens within ourselves and in the community. *The mystery of suffering proves to be a profound pathway into a participatory experience with God!*

What God has done and is doing through our Lord Jesus Christ unfolds inexplicably in and through suffering. The community itself comes about through the suffering of Christ. In turn, suffering is often lived in and through the church (Colossians 1:24). Suffering is not on the periphery of our life together. Indeed, it is at the very core of the community's origin and life.

So a healthy community teaches us how to hold suffering in innumerable ways. We bear one another's burdens. We share in the fellowship of suffering. We participate in this life together of death and dying. This is done again and again and again. It marks us. It distinguishes us as God's people. As the community teaches us, we then are "able to comfort those who are in any affliction" (2 Corinthians 1:4 ESV).

For informing and strengthening a particular character.
True-self living is not simply a matter of feeling connected or
close in the good times and in the bad. Nor is it only a matter
of like-mindedness because we affirm a common set of beliefs
or convictions (such as the Apostles' Creed or the Westminster Confession). The Christian community also participates in and cultivates a shared character. True-self living may
or may not foster times of rewarding communion with God
and unity of experience with fellow believers. But it always
fosters a way of being that involves virtues. Together we have
the chance to become more virtuous.

Character is not embracing moral platitudes or virtuous
ways of acting. Jesus isn't interested in his church putting on
virtues as if wearing a garment. His concern is that we are
formed internally in such a way that we are literally structured in and by certain virtues. His goal for us is that we
become moral persons from the inside out, not simply that we
do virtuous things.

The false self is adept at adopting morals that look appropriate and lead to social approval while having no depth of
character within the soul. It is the essential danger of anyone
who seeks to live a godly life. Morality can be merely part of
an image. This was the righteousness of the Pharisees in Jesus'
day. They had a form of morality that led to religious and
social rules. Their righteousness was understood as following
the rules, keeping the code of conduct.

Jesus said something different. According to him our character is to be profoundly internal, a matter of the heart (Mark
7:20-23). Building on this interior orientation of moral character the apostle Paul spoke of the virtues of the Christian as

fruit of the Spirit (Galatians 5:22). The presence of God's Spirit resident within the souls of God's people should bear an internal moral orientation. This type of character is an interior reality that structures the soul to be a certain type of person. God is not nurturing a people who simply *act* patient or kind. He is nurturing people who *are* patient and kind. With this orientation we can follow our hearts rather than simply focusing on how we behave.

We learn this way of deep interior moral being by participating in a community of relational communion. It is not possible to learn it any other way. The relational participation that marks the community then provides an opportunity for our permeable souls to internalize this profoundly interior way of virtuous living. This virtuous character then finds itself creatively expressed in behavior that bears the likeness of Christ.

For humility and gratitude. If we are attentive to this way of living in a community of faith, we will find ourselves formed by two primary virtues—humility and gratitude. Humility is the realization that a true-self life is beyond our capability. By ourselves we cannot generate radical moral interiority. In fact we realize matters of morality are easily co-opted by our false self. It distorts issues of morality either by privatizing all moral issues so that we actually have little accountability except to our own notions of good and evil (which, by the way, are easily skewed) or by insulating the soul with a self-centeredness that prohibits any real exercise of self-examination deep within the heart. On the one hand our false self can justify just about anything; on the other it can repress the deeper issues of the heart, making morality a superficial matter.

Humility is the virtue that confronts our exaggerated privatization as well as our superficial platitudes. It postures the soul in dependency on God by opening the soul to Scripture and Spirit. Humility ultimately says, "Thy will be done." Humility ushers in a life of confession and repentance. Repentance without humility is artificial self-righteousness that will never expose the deep motivations of the soul. True humility leads both individually and as a community to openheartedness and truth telling.

The community also lives with a profound sense of gratitude. God in his mercy awaits us. Whenever we turn toward him, he welcomes us home. He forgives us. There is no condemnation in Christ (Romans 8:1), only the profound relationship of being in Christ as sons and daughters of the Father. It is only reasonable that our hearts are filled with thanksgiving.

Of the practice of gratitude Alan Jones writes, "In our work together, we've come to focus on developing and using a practice of gratitude. . . . The first step on this path is recognizing that gratitude isn't just an exercise of etiquette: one more virtue we should cultivate. . . . Rather, it is our spontaneous response when we wake up to that fact that life is a gift."[4] The life we live, a life of participation in God and community, is pure gift. Humility postures us to receive it. Gratitude is the posture once we have received it.

BRINGING IT HOME TO OUR HEARTS

Rachel's life was transformed in community. There she learned to trust God and others. There she learned a different way of being. There she learned the virtues of humility and gratitude. It didn't happen by reading a book. Her transformation took place *because* she was in a healthy community.

Sadly, some have had a very different experience in community. Rather than a transformation of soul, they have experienced a deformation of soul. They entered a community hoping to find a home of unconditional love. What they found was a self-righteous, self-protective, self-promoting reality. If this has been your experience, we are truly sorry. But the fact that communities often fail to live into what the gospel makes possible is no reason to reject community. The emergence of our true self depends on the community life we live in. It is critical that we all find a good church so that our true self can flourish.

Jesus commanded us to love God with all our heart, soul, mind and strength, and to love our neighbor as ourself (Matthew 22:37-40). These are not commands randomly fished out of a repository of sage advice. They are the ways by which the very structure of our true self comes to life. If we, by God's grace, are to live a true-self life and experience soulful relationships with others, we too must not take for granted our privilege of living among other Christians. We must engage the invitation and reality of life together as children of God. The people, the Word, the prayers, the sacraments and the worship call me to live beyond myself, to live *by* community, *for* community.

As we live in a healthy community we will develop a greater capacity to trust. The community will have fostered a deeper faith in the triune God. In turn, faith fosters the freedom that empowers individuals to surrender. As we surrender we are less preoccupied with ourselves and able to show up in real ways for others. We will be less reactive and more receptive. Community is a grand invitation to surrender, which, at its core, is an invitation to trust. Since trust is at the heart of true-self living we can truthfully say that such a life is impossible apart from community.

FOR REFLECTION AND DISCUSSION

1. Why has God always acted in and through a particular kind of community? How has the community of faith helped you grow toward soulful relationships?

2. Why is surrender so important in the life of a community and the cultivation of soulful relationships? What might God be inviting you to relinquish as a result of your life in community?

3. How do the particulars of the communities you live in serve as means of maturation and growth? What things are challenging for you? What is God's invitation for you in this challenge?

4. What idealized expectations do you have of others that may be hindering your entering into a deeper relational communion?

5. How does understanding our suffering as participation in the life of Christ recalibrate how we see our world? How has suffering shaped your relationships with God and others?

6. What is the relationship between vulnerability and suffering? What is the relationship between trust and suffering?

7. Why do you think God instructs us to bear one another's burdens? How might you cultivate soulful relationships as you help bear the burdens of others?

9

CORE SPIRITUAL DISCIPLINES

Engaging with God

Jonathan has been a business leader in his community for almost thirty years. Though the success of his company kept him very busy, he made time to serve as a deacon or elder in his church. He also served his community through various committees in city government. Jonathan had a life he could and should be proud of. He was respected and loved by his family, friends, employees and church family. He maintained regular practices of prayer and Scripture reading over the course of many years. But now these disciplines had become pretty sporadic. A general malaise had settled over Jonathan, and he wasn't sure what to do to move past his feelings of being stuck.

Sometimes when we feel we are not moving forward in emotionally fulfilling ways we need to take a step back and focus on the basics of relational engagement. That is what Jonathan felt he should do. He knew his relationship with God needed both space and intentionality. So he returned to the spiritual disciplines of solitude and silence. "I scheduled times where I was alone and quiet for a few minutes each day. I took short walks in the forest preserve that is close to my work and just imagined myself walking quietly with Jesus. I began to read a few verses from the Gospels and reflect on the story of Jesus as if it were written just to me."

After a couple months he noticed a shift in his soul. In listening to God and his own soul during his prayer walks Jonathan noticed old memories that troubled him. He was surprised that the loss of his younger brother to a tragic drowning accident provoked such deep emotion of sorrow on one occasion. "I had thought of Dan's death from time to time but always believed God had a purpose I would never understand. But on my walks I couldn't stop crying. I really have missed my brother."

At fifty-one Jonathan came home to himself in a new and powerful way. In his times of solitude and silence he revisited the loss of his brother and all that he had missed without his presence. By doing a life map he was able to explore more fully his feelings and his relationships in his family of origin. He integrated more deeply in his soul what he had lived. As he grew in self-clarity he found his times with God to be more real. He also became less driven by compulsive feelings of guilt to do more.

When asked what had happened Jonathan reflected, "I didn't have some exhilarating spiritual experience. But slowly things changed for me. I'm definitely more settled within my soul, and I feel more present to my wife and kids and even to God. I'm just living more open to God, myself and others. In fact my wife mentioned that I'm less defensive when talking to her than I used to be. She's pretty glad about that!"

Jonathan found that he became more trusting and thus more receptive. In coming home to God more honestly he was coming home to himself. He was living more from his true self. His journey of faith took a turn when he intentionally engaged in some different but time-honored spiritual disciplines.

FOUR DISCIPLINES OF SOULFUL RELATIONSHIPS

Soulful relationships are a gift anchored in our life in Christ. But this gift doesn't appear out of thin air. It comes to us when we make room for it. To put it another way, *soulful relationships are a gift that requires our intentionality.* We know this to be true. A strong marriage and a solid family is the fruit of someone being intentional. Someone has made certain choices and has practiced certain skills like waiting, listening, clearly expressing needs and desires, storytelling, patience, repentance and a good dose of self-knowledge.

Strong relationships are the fruit of doing certain things well. They are like the harvest the farmer gains after hard work. No farmer can make the sun shine, the rain fall or the seed sprout. But the farmer can and must plow and plant, hoe and harvest. When it comes to enjoying soulful relationships—relationships marked by love, graciousness, honesty, understanding, loyalty and vulnerability—certain things have to be practiced in order for the soul to mature into these character traits. Jonathan's story illustrates this reality. He became intentional and sought to live more consistently in time-honored spiritual practices that formed the soul toward deeper communion with God and others.

Our conviction is that there are four indispensable spiritual disciplines that foster soulful relationships: solitude, silence, contemplative reading of Scripture and contemplative prayer. These disciplines prepare the soil of the soul for the seed of life God longs to give. They are means by which God's people have fallen in love with God and matured in Christ. There are many other Christian spiritual disciplines.[1] But we are convinced that these four disciplines are critical for soulful relationships, and so we want to consider them in this chapter. Without intentionally incorporating them in our life we will find our relationships diminished.

One final word before individually exploring these disciplines—spiritual disciplines are not an end in themselves. They are a means to an end. They facilitate an awakening to what is most real. Disciplines set the soul on the path where it can come to know God and live present to others in love. If disciplines become the end game, they will become empty rituals that will leave the soul narrowed and parched.

Solitude. Many of us are neurotically busy. We live with limited time and emotional margins because we are compulsively driven. There is money to be made, ministry to be done, people to see and places to go. We live in a culture that becomes anxious if things get too quiet. So we live with a TV or radio playing. It's hard to stay away from checking the news or playing a game on our smartphones. We are afraid to slow down, afraid to still our hearts, afraid to be silent, afraid to be alone. And if we get the space for solitude, there is little appetite for it because we feel guilty or ashamed when we are not busy.

Solitude is a simple discipline. Most of us could find a place to be alone and quiet. But the aloneness and stillness proves difficult. We feel we should do something even when we are alone and quiet. When we try to practice solitude, we discover how addicted we are to our compulsive busyness. But this is precisely why we need to accept the invitation of Scripture to "wait quietly before God" (Psalm 62:1).

Solitude leads us into a space where we are alone, a space without clutter, congestion and demands. We are still and quiet. Soulful relationships require this kind of space. *It is impossible to be with someone if we are not able to be with ourselves.* Solitude forces us to be with ourselves.

The danger of our compulsive doing is that we avoid our own souls. We live busy, scurrying from ourselves. We then live on the fringe of our souls and settle for the trite and the trivial. Solitude brings us home to ourselves, home to our own souls. I (Rich) recall a conversation with a pastor who was very successful in building his church. But his marriage was hurting. I asked him, "Who are you apart from your pastoral work?" He looked at me, frowned and said, "Could you repeat the question?" I did. He pondered the question a long time and finally replied, "I don't understand the question." And he didn't understand because he had no idea of who he was apart from his work. He was like many of us, clueless about who we are apart from what we do and how we perform. We wind up being the image of our busyness. This is why we desperately need solitude.

When we engage in this discipline it is not unusual to feel a nagging level of anxiety. We don't know what to do with our pain, brokenness, incompleteness, limits and losses. If we are not intentional with solitude this pain will drive us further into our compulsive busyness.

We must come home to our own soul, our pain, our limits and our losses if we are to engage more deeply in true-self living. We must give our soul time to grieve. We can't keep trying to escape our own life. The life we have is the life we've got. It is the only life we will ever have. Solitude provides the space to come home to our selves and to our pain.

Silence. Silence is the twin of solitude. It is hardly worth our while to be alone in a clutter of noise. We need quiet. Our souls need the stilling of multitude sounds so they can breathe deeply. But it is not easy to silence our surroundings. For most of us we have to intentionally extricate ourselves from the loudness of life so we can enter a silent space.

However, the silence we need is not only a quiet external space. The discipline of silence includes the cultivation of an inner quietness as well. This can prove more difficult than finding a quiet place in a city. We are busy brained, always thinking, processing, reflecting, analyzing, plotting, strategizing, listing, ordering, figuring and dreaming. Our minds jump from one thought to another in a millisecond. Thomas Keating calls it monkey mind. We swing from limb to limb in our heads.

Getting the monkeys to calm down takes a rhythm of solitude and silence. But if practiced long enough we will experience a stilling of our mind so that we can engage our emotions held in our implicit memory. This is vitally important because soulful relationships foster a settledness within the soul. Life-giving relationships are not built on how smart we are but on how solid we are. This is not to diminish the capacities of cognition and communication. They are part of what it means to be created in the image of God. But we are more than our thoughts and words. Our soul has terrain that is deeper than what we think. In this terrain of the soul there is knowledge of truth, love and mercy that is far more than mere information.[2]

The soul's deepest terrain is not experienced by more thinking or doing, but by means of solitude and silence. Our thoughts are often ways we try to control things. There is much in life that needs our control. But in our most significant relationships we must relinquish control as a way to trust more deeply.

Solitude and silence facilitate a way of knowing that transcends thinking. In solitude and silence we know ourselves and are known by God at a profound level. In time, solitude and silence lead us into the deeper terrain of our soul. There we find levels of anxiety, guilt, shame and pain staring us in the face. We meet our limits and losses in profound ways. We encounter our brokenness and our weakness. This can make us more anxious than we want to be. But as we meet all of who we are, we begin to realize how we have used everything at our disposal to control our lives. Exaggerated control is the enemy of trust. It generates more reactivity rather than receptivity.

Coming home to this deeper soul terrain is painful. We do it like the prodigal son in Luke 15. We come to our senses. We return to our Father in humility and weakness. Thankfully, he welcomes us home with open arms. In God's receptive grace the soul enters the terrain of knowing it is born of love and lives in love. The soul is truly home because God created us to enjoy the gift of trusting, loving relationships.

Without solitude and silence much of our religious activity is merely a false-self project. Without a healthy dose of solitude and silence our ubiquitous and powerful false self co-opts our spirituality in service of the agendas of our ego. Without solitude and silence we wind up spiritualizing our compulsions. This is why so many of us find our souls tired and drained in midlife. The strategies of the false self eventually collapse under the strain and pressure of life. The oxygen for soulful relationships is solitude and silence experiencing the healing presence of the Father, Son and Spirit.

Contemplative reading of Scripture. The third discipline is contemplative reading of Scripture. This skill plays a vital part in the maturing of the soul. Unfortunately, we are swimming upstream with this discipline as well. Most of our training and practice of reading in our educational experience has been for the purpose of mastering material and increasing our knowledge (and thus control). We have done this for so long that we believe reading for mastery is the only kind of reading there is. It isn't.

Contemplative reading of Scripture is structured so that instead of gaining mastery of the text we are mastered. Instead of increasing our competency, we are encouraged to surrender in humility. Indeed, instead of reading the text, we hope to be read by the text. It is the journey of placing our story into God's story. The goal of contemplative reading is *not* the amassing of knowledge but the reinterpretation of our story so that it is congruent with the truth of God's story.

Through contemplative reading we long to encounter God's truth. Our souls often resist truth because we are self-protective and self-preserving. The thing that can mature us is a deep trust in the living God. Such trust makes the soul more open, more receptive to what God has to say. Reality is created by God's word. And God's Word illumines the path to what is life's truest reality. That is where we want to live. The more we are grasped by the Word and Truth made flesh, the greater will be our capacity to engage in deep abiding relational intimacy.

Table 1 charts the different ways we might read God's Word. Each way is significant and has its place in the life of a mature person of faith.

Table 1. From Factual to Contemplative

Factual	Theological	Devotional	Contemplative
Information	Inspiration	Motivation	Transformation
Propositions learned	Promises believed	Principles embodied	Presence encountered
Knowing the truth of God	Exploring the revelation of God	Living the life of God	Enjoying the person of God

Contemplative reading is a way of hearing God's voice, encountering God's presence through Scripture so we can experience and enjoy communion and transformation. We are not looking to the Bible to find solutions to our problems (for example, getting a list of verses dealing with worry or depression). Nor are we coming to Scripture for a message or devotional to share with others. We are simply listening to God.

It is possible to study the Bible without ever encountering the living God. This is what happened to the Pharisees. They studied but missed the point of Scripture, which is an encounter with Jesus (John 5:39). Without the Spirit of Christ the Bible is not a life-giving word. The signs and symbols of words on a page have life only in that they point toward what is alive and true. Contemplative reading of the Scripture is a way of seeking the God behind (but not contrary to) the words. It is based on the promise that God reveals himself to all who seek him (1 Chronicles 28:9) and that to find God is to find our true self in Christ.

Thus the goal of contemplative reading is twofold: first, to confront us with the truth of our own existence (by breaking down our spiritual, psychological and behavior barriers) so that we show up as we really are in the presence of God, not as we project ourselves to be (not in our false self); second, to find ourselves in the very presence of the living God whose presence transforms our souls.

Contemplative reading is not magical (though it is in some sense mystical). It is not a method or technique. It is a way by which we descend from the level of our head, through our heart, to the depths of our soul to discover our true selves in Christ through the Holy Spirit. The assumption behind this kind of reading is that the Bible is the inspired Word of God and that its intent is to communicate the heart of God. Contemplative reading trusts the Spirit to bring that Word to us in a way that is life giving, in a way that brings us into the transforming presence of Christ.

The *first* movement of contemplative reading is the actual *reading* of Scripture (*lectio*). We start with a brief prayer asking God to help us be present to the Spirit and the Scripture. Then we read the short selection of Scripture slowly, repeatedly and out loud. As we read it a second, third and fourth time we allow our imagination to locate us in what we are reading.

In this kind of reading the Spirit of Christ often brings us to a meaning that lies beyond the surface (literal) meaning of the text (as a lover can convey more to his or her beloved than what the words used are literally saying). So we listen with open hearts for a loving word that pulls us into the story.

The *second* movement is *reflecting* (*meditatio*) on what we have read. The first step of repeated reading involves placing ourselves in the Scripture by means of our imagination. The second step is more a matter of meditating on what lies beneath the surface of our lives that is responding to the Scripture. We pay attention to what is rising in our souls. We allow the text to trigger memories and associations deep within us.

It is crucial that we sit with whatever arises in us as we reflect. It may be sorrow, satisfaction, emptiness, fullness, anger, resentment, joy or hope. Whatever it is, we don't try to solve or resolve it. We give it the honor and respect it deserves because it is a part of us. Sitting without judgment on what arises gives the Spirit permission to continue exploring what is hidden to us. Sometimes it is helpful to ask ourselves questions like, What kind of God would be saying this to me? or, How does what I am feeling impact my relationship with God and others?

The *third* movement is *responding* (*oratio*). But our response is not a matter of deciding to do something when we are done with our reading. Instead it is a prayer for clarity, for illumination of what has stirred in us. Whatever has risen to the surface needs to be interpreted by God's love and purpose for us.

The one who loves more sees more. (Love is a form of knowledge.) As we respond with a prayer for understanding, God begins to show us what has been acting below the surface of our souls. As we see this we surrender our false self into the loving hand of God. In this way God works to reform and transform our souls so that our unhealthy defenses and attachment patterns, our exaggerated responses and false-self strategies progressively give way to our true self in Christ. We must be mindful of our tendency to find a quick resolution to what the Spirit has revealed by judging, blaming, withdrawing or resolving. This is something we must learn to resist. We want to learn to trust that God is greater than anything in us. God is up to the task of transformation. "God, who began the good work within you, will continue his work until it is finally finished" (Philippians 1:6). Nothing in us can overcome his love for us in Christ (Romans 8:38).

The *fourth* movement in contemplative reading is *resting* (*contemplatio*). It is a willingness to embrace God's invitation in light of how God's story affects our story. This is probably the step most difficult to describe and enter. It is moving beyond words to a kind of communion where no words are needed.

As we rest in God there is less intellectual reasoning and a greater awareness of our longing to be loved and to love. Here our false self, with its autonomy, self-sufficiency and compulsive habits of exercising control, begins to give way to the presence of the love of God for and in us. Now nothing else really matters anymore. As we rest in God we find we are drawn deeper into what is truest about us. We are drawn more and more into our true self in Christ. We are stirred by the power of the love of Christ.

Contemplative reading is a means by which God's loving presence is experienced and expressed in our mortal bodies. It is one of the ways God exposes our false self so that we can surrender it and live more into our true self in Christ. It is a way by which we grow in compassion for others, because by it we enter the freedom of Christ's love.

Contemplative reading is essential for soulful relationships because it is an experience where God's story engages our story. What is false is exposed. What is true is awakened and enlivened by God's Spirit. In the deeper terrain of our soul we find we are more receptive to God and others and ourselves by the Spirit.

Contemplative prayer. We turn now to the fourth essential discipline that fosters soulful relationships—contemplative prayer. There are many types of prayers (such as intercession, thanksgiving or confession). What distinguishes contemplative prayer from other forms of prayer is a listening posture. Like contemplative reading (where the reader seeks more to be read than to read) contemplative prayer seeks more to listen than to speak. Consequently, in contemplative prayer there are fewer words and more silence than in other prayers.

In contemplative prayer we are heeding the counsel of David: "Be still, and know that I am God!" (Psalm 46:10). Contemplative prayer is a willingness to enjoy and be present to God. *It is a matter of being consciously aware of my presence in Christ and attentive to Christ's presence within me.* It is saying yes to God with my whole being but without words. "It is a careful attentiveness to the One who dwells in the center of our being such that through the recognition of God's presence we allow God to take possession of all our senses."[3]

Christian contemplative prayer is not to be confused with Eastern meditative practices of emptying the mind so that the meditator can enter the oneness (or nothingness) of the universe. Contemplative prayer is a willingness to present all we are to the triune God. We are not losing ourselves in a vast impersonal force. We are coming home to the personal God, who loves us in his Son through his Spirit. Contemplative prayer is a way of being in relationship with the presence of God *within* me through the person of the Holy Spirit.

Most of us know how to pray with words. Often we find praying without words to be difficult. But our souls need this experience. It is good for us to be so present to God that nothing needs or can be spoken. In a place of quiet communion the false self is confronted with the presence of Christ. Contemplative prayer is that powerful discipline that undermines our illusion of control. It is an *intention* of being with God and God alone for the sake of love.

Maybe it's because we've both cleared the sixty-year mark that we feel we have said just about enough to God. We find that we have repeated the same thing again and again in our prayers. Frankly, we are quickly bored with our words! So we feel we need to listen more. We feel the need to be more quiet in his presence. In saying this we are not making a case to abandon words in prayer. Speaking to God quietly in our hearts or even verbally is significant and important. Words make our longings and desires specific and concrete. We need words in prayer. But words, as important as they are, restrict, limit, confine and even may corrupt love. Try as I (Rich) might to put the delightful play of my grandchildren into words, something is lost. No words can express the depth of this love. Soulful relationships live in this love, long for this love, rest in this love. They need the space and confidence to be able to be with another in silence.

The truth is that this sort of empty space makes us anxious, at least in the beginning of the relationship. Maybe this is why newlyweds talk endlessly! But over time, when there is a maturing love in marriage or friendship, a growing space of silence develops. Has love ended because there are no words? No. The relationship has simply grown to a point where fewer words are needed. Contemplative prayer allows the soul to learn of a love that is beyond words. Contemplative prayer nudges us to wake up to what is most real.

Again, words matter, and there are times to speak in prayer. We get that. What we are saying, however, is that most of us are addicted to words. The soul desperately needs to learn a communion without words. We long for this communion in the deepest terrain of our soul. The soul longs to live from this place! This is contemplative prayer communion without words.

Bringing It Home to Our Hearts

Perhaps you are experiencing something like Jonathan did. You may not be sure of what it is, but you sense something is missing in this stage of your journey. If so we invite you to consider becoming more intentional with the four contemplative disciplines. Don't be discouraged if you find yourself restless or anxious. If you, like Jonathan, are remembering experiences that are hard for you to process alone, then find someone who will listen to your story. Begin the journey. A deeper communion is available. God is delighted that you are willing!

For Reflection and Discussion

1. Does Jonathan's experience ring true for you? If so, what do you feel is missing from your relationship with God?

2. Which of the four disciplines seems to tug at your heart the most? Why do you think this is so?

3. Which of these disciplines seems most difficult or improbable for you and why? What are you noticing about what you think and feel regarding this discipline?

4. What disciplines have you practiced that you find nurture soulful relationships? Which of the disciplines do you need to practice for cultivating soulful relationships?

5. How would you express the conviction that the practice of these disciplines leads to soulful relationships? Why do you believe this is true?

6. How might you begin to implement the practice of these disciplines more intentionally?

7. At this stage in reading the book, what have you learned about soulful relationships? How would you describe your relationship with God at this juncture of your faith journey?

10

Transformation

Changing the Way We Live

Recently a young pastor asked, "Does anyone really change? And if they do, what does it look like?" Because we knew his story, we had an idea of the frustration that led to his questions. He loved Jesus and believed the gospel. But he found himself struggling with the same relational stuff he had for years. "I honestly wonder if I am really becoming someone different. I don't really love or connect in the way I want."

We have asked the same questions of ourselves and felt the same discouragement as our friend. His questions and ours were part of the motivation for this book. We have preached many sermons, led many retreats and counseled and coached many leaders. And more important, we have taken long looks at our own failures and struggles. Is major change possible, or is minor tinkering the best we can hope for? We know in Christ we are "a new creation" and "the old life is gone; the new life has begun" (2 Corinthians 5:17). We believe this is true, but it certainly doesn't mean everything about us is different, because Scripture also says we are being changed "from one degree of glory to another" (2 Corinthians 3:18 ESV). What then is realistic? How much can we really change?

Back in my (Rich) early thirties, after having been a pastor for a dozen years or so, one of my mentors said, "If you really desire to stay healthy in the Christian life, you will need to develop a working understanding of adult transformation." Thirty years later I couldn't agree more. If we are going to make it in life, we need a clear understanding of adult change. Without this we will become discouraged and frustrated with ourselves and others.

THE TRUTH ABOUT CHANGE

The truth about significant soul transformation is this—change is possible, but it is harder than we want and takes longer than we expect. Can we learn to trust God, others and ourselves in ways that bring life? Yes. But . . .

We first need to be clear about what God is out to change. Recently, we listened to a bright, attractive woman sobbing deeply, and between gasps for breath she whispered, "I hate myself. I hate everything about who I am." Her words were filled with the enormous pain of a soul immersed in shame's self-contempt. She wanted everything, literally everything, about her to be different—the color of her hair and eyes, the shape of her lips and hips, her height and weight, her family and friends.

While this is a rather extreme example, the truth is that many of us have grandiose expectations about what we think should change. We want change where change isn't needed or expected by God. *We miss or ignore that God is out to change our capacity to love and be loved.* In other words, God is seeking to change the posture of our hearts from mistrust to trust. God is transforming us from a heart curved inward on itself to a heart that is more open to God and others.

Why is this change harder than we want it to be? Simply put, change is challenging because of our soul's stubbornness. We have learned a way to be me that is enduring and resistant to change. Granted, there are developmental changes unfolding through various life stages, but even in developmental changes there is an enduring me.

We all have ways of thinking, feeling, evaluating, deciding, desiring and behaving. And the way we do these becomes habitual. They are anchored in psychological structures that are held in implicit memory (in our pattern of relational attachment). A lot of me is outside of my conscious awareness, much like an old habit. My me feels comfortable and safe (even though others may see it as severely dysfunctional). And so it is hard to see what needs changing, and even if we can see it we cannot directly change it because the structures of me are buried deeply in the implicit world.

When we become aware of the deeper terrain of our soul, the arena of our implicit memory, we begin to understand that real change requires more than willpower and easy, simple steps. We cannot rescue ourselves. There are no shortcuts, no easy paths and no quick fixes. The more mature we are in our Christian faith, the more aware we are of the depth of change needed within our souls. From a practical point of view, anyone who has attempted to change harsh, negative self-talk, reactive anger, feelings of worthlessness, a preoccupation with pornography, a persistent grumpy attitude or persistent feelings of frustration understands that real soul transformation is not simple. If we are going to substantially change, something will have to die. But our false self never volunteers for its funeral.

WHY SO LONG?

Change is possible, but it is harder than we imagined and takes longer than we want. Why does it take so long? Why doesn't God do something miraculous so we don't have to struggle so?

The good news is that God has done something miraculous. We had alienated ourselves from God by refusing to trust his goodness, by failing to participate in his life. And there was nothing we could do to change that. So God became one of us to redeem us and show us the way to live fully human (by completely trusting the Father). The Word became flesh and dwelled among us (John 1:14). By faith in him we are born anew into the likeness of Christ by the Holy Spirit (John 1:12-13; 3:16; 1 Peter 1:3).

But there is still work to do. The new birth makes possible a new life. But this life will take a lifetime to unfold. God's grace and Spirit work through the natural order God has established to nurture us into the likeness of Christ. God most often works through the natural process of our healing as we learn and develop new levels of awareness and skills. That means we must address issues of attachment and the like. And that takes a long time. So we do well to disabuse ourselves of simplistic approaches to God's work of transformation. We do well to engage the journey of transformation with sobermindedness and a firm hope in the living presence of God within us. After all, any change is miraculous no matter how long it takes.

When it comes to real change, the operative word is *patience*, a willingness to stay the course and recognize that in my ordinary life God is present and at work. Within everyday living, our life story is unfolding within God's story. To move too quickly would be to lose ourselves.

What Is Ours

We need to have realistic expectations if we are going to engage a journey of real-life change. Our false self resists true change. Our culture shows little interest in helping us with real change. We have an enemy who seeks our demise (Ephesians 6:12; 1 Peter 5:8). So there is much working against us. But there is one who came to liberate us. He brings us back into fellowship with the Father. He sets us free from our self-serving bondage and the power of sin and all its varied forms of enduring entanglements. By faith Christ is in us and we are in him. His life is our life. This is not simply an idea. It is an actuality and the essence of our life. The presence of the living God is within us.

Numerous benefits are ours because of the presence of Christ in us. His righteousness, his life, his victory over sin and death, his communion with the Father are all ours. In Christ, God is for us. God welcomes us home to his presence. We are embraced as his very own adopted children. We are no longer alienated from God, from others or from ourselves. We are set free to live from our giftedness.

Ours is a new life, an eternal life, the very life of God. In the soul's deepest terrain God in Christ has wrought a radical change. In Christ there is a change in our identity, in our motivation, in our desire, in our values, in our destiny. The essence of who we are is found in Christ. At the center of who we are, both in and beneath conscious awareness, Christ has entered, and his life is now ours. Whatever my egoic habits might be, Christ lives beneath them and his presence is at work to disempower them over time. Nothing of the me that I am will be left untouched by Christ's presence. Even the deepest psychological distortions, the most tenacious foul attitude or the most stubborn behavior habit will give way to Christ someday.

We must never lose sight of the truth that Christ lives in us and our life is hidden in him (Colossians 3:3). We must learn to embrace this truth, drink this truth, sit in stillness with this truth, wrestle with this truth and finally surrender all that we are to this truth. It must permeate the deepest recesses of our soul. The God who lives within holds all things together, even our frayed, distorted, broken realities. Because he loves us, we can surrender everything we are to him, embracing the gift that we are. Change is often delayed and derailed because we are afraid, too preoccupied with our ego's need to control. Instead we can trust that surrender is our best option. Then change will come. God will do it. We don't muster up the energy to change. Instead, we rest in the life that is ours in Christ.

THE RELATIONAL SOUL

The way of transformation that leads to soulful relationships is through dying and rising with Christ. We surrender to his life. His way becomes our way. Without a death, new life is impossible. If nothing dies, we are left holding on to our false-self way of doing life. We will have no choice but to cling to our defenses, our point of view, our theology, our political party, our favorite institutions, our sports team. This will leave us brittle and easily offended.

When God in his grace visits us, something must give. We no longer can hold on to it all. The pain is often sharp and penetrates deeply. We feel confused and dazed. Our point of reference for being who we are can be lost or clouded. We may enter a "dark night of the soul." But after the dying there is a birth. In the center of our soul a freedom, a wider heart, a softer presence, a more resilient self begins to emerge. Our true self shows itself.

The following are five distinct characteristics we will begin to notice as we surrender to Christ. They are openness, awareness, curiosity, acceptance and forgiveness. These mark a receptive, trusting heart. They are part of the essential mystery of our souls becoming Christlike. They make soulful relationships possible. They are at the heart of true-self living.

Openness of heart. The presence of Christ fosters within us an openheartedness, the willingness to receive and to give. Often there is an emphasis on how we should give ourselves to others. While that is true, we must always remember that we learn to give love by first receiving love. Often too little attention is given to the need of an open heart to receive love. Maybe it is because living openheartedly is risky. It demands vulnerability and humility. Our pride is like that of the two-year-old who says, "I do it!" Our self-protective instincts born of our inherent shame, fear and guilt resist an open heart. In addition we can point to experiences with people where we were hurt deeply. So we live protected, cautious, all-too-careful lives.

Jesus lived differently. He was open to setting aside divine prerogatives, to emptying himself and to becoming a servant (Philippians 2:1-11). He humbled himself. He was open to mothers bringing their infants, villagers bringing the broken, disciples bringing their fears, friends bearing their sorrow, and a dying thief's desperate plea. He was open to all who came to him, even the wrong kind of people. At the end of his life he was open to his Father's will of death on a cross. His openness was not the result of the absence of convictions or deeply held values. Jesus clearly had boundaries and limits. His life demonstrates that openness is not spineless tolerance. But what his life shows is an attitude of receptivity, a willingness to welcome who and what was brought to him as if they were brought to him by his heavenly Father.

A life of openness is a life of faith. It is the willingness to live with a heart vulnerable to the love of another. It is a willingness to listen, to hear someone out, to consider a different perspective, to ruminate and contemplate, and to seek further understanding. It is a willingness to be less protected by the strategies in our implicit memory.

Soulful relationships are nurtured in a love that receives openheartedly and gives in return. One of the fruits of change is the willingness and expression of openness. It is proof that our capacity to trust is growing. Such openness is anchored in God's love for us in Christ. It is not for the faint of heart or for mere curiosity seekers. Openness of heart is for those willing to embrace painful transformation. When the psalmist cried, "Search me, O God, and know my heart," he opened his soul (Psalm 139:23). He was willing to be known, to be exposed.

Attentiveness of heart. Attentiveness is the capacity to notice things, the ability to see what is really happening. It is the power to observe without becoming swept up in judgment or reactivity. Attentiveness expands our awareness and broadens our depth of life. Leighton Ford defines attentiveness as "respecting, attending to, waiting on, looking at and listening to the other—the persons and things that we encounter—for what they are in themselves, not what we can make of them."[1]

There is no better literary record of being attentive than Anne Dillard's work *Pilgrim at Tinker Creek*. In really noticing her surroundings she became aware of a world teaming with complexity, fecundity and God's holy presence. Everyday life was brimming over before her eyes. She only needed to be attentive. And as she noticed life more profoundly, there was a change in her connections with God and others.

Being attentive to God happens when we are willing to be attentive to what is actually in our lives. In the unfolding of the ordinary and seemingly mundane details of our lives, God visits us. Earthy, sober-minded attentiveness will bring us home to ourselves. Instead of living in the images we create or our culture creates for us, we live from the core of what is real about ourselves and others.

The psalmist prayed that that God would keep him from presumptuous sins (Psalm 19:13). He did not want to live blindly, indulging in sins born from inattention and cluelessness. Instead, he longed to live from a posture of profound attentiveness that gives birth to awareness. This is precisely what Jesus did. He paid attention to what was happening around him with great openness of soul. He told his followers that if they could see well they would be healthy (Luke 11:34).

When we are inattentive we are distracted. We then center our souls on the peripheral and secondary. We need constant reminders to pay attention. While teaching me to fly in northern Ontario, my (Jim) flight instructors constantly said, "Pay attention." While flying on skis in the winter, I had to pay attention to snow drifts and slush on the ice. While flying on floats in the summer, I had to pay attention to the impact of waves or a log in the water. Not taking something into account could easily result in a wreck. While hunting for our meat, my dad reminded my brother and me to pay careful attention. Before pulling the trigger we had to be sure it was a moose in the woods and not one of us. Not paying attention could lead to serious consequences with a high-powered rifle.

All of us are tempted to let our minds wander. Our "oughts" and "shoulds" distract us. Our past and future distract us. Our compulsiveness born of exaggerated shame, fear and guilt distracts us from ourselves and others. As a consequence our relationships suffer because our souls suffer from lack of attentiveness. Instead of hearing others we project our unresolved interior world on others. As we live in the love of Christ we receive the gift of maturing attentiveness. We increasingly become more aware of what matters. We are able to see and hear matters of the heart. When someone speaks, we notice. When someone is silent, we hear.

All true repentance and our capacity to clearly and correctly identify the idols of our hearts is a direct result of openheartedness and attentiveness to God's Spirit. Repentance disconnected from openheartedness and awareness will be at best shallow or at worst a spiritual idol of self-righteousness.

All deep turning from pride and selfish preoccupation issues from a heart open to the living presence of God and attentive to what is true about our soul.

Attentiveness of heart cannot help but lead to soulful relationships. We become more aware and integrated persons by attentiveness. We become more grounded in ourselves, and our wholeness enables us to be more fully present to those we love and the God who daily invites us deeper into communion with him. We live less from a fabricated, fragmented and fragile reality. We live more from the core identity in Christ, who dwells within us.

Curiosity of heart. Curiosity is the inquisitive willingness to explore. It recognizes there is more to life than what meets the eye. Curiosity builds on the foundation of openness and attentiveness. This posture of soul isn't just for children. It is for friends who are committed to nurturing their relationship. It is for married persons wanting to deepen their love. It is for parents eager to shape and fashion children into mature and responsible adults. It is for middle-age adults seeking to nurture new ways of living simply and creatively while avoiding the pitfalls of boredom and midlife reactivity. It is for grandparents seeking to learn how best to love the next generation. It is for seniors desiring to finish life with joy and meaning. It is for all of us who long to live wholeheartedly into the likeness of Christ.

Curiosity is indispensable for fostering soulful relationships. Apathy and indifference erodes life within our relationships. All around us are people filled with mystery waiting to be discovered. Persons who are no longer curious abandon a gift from God that fosters growth and maturation.

I (Rich) remember visiting the homes of persons attending our church in the beginning of my years of pastoral ministry. I was usually anxious, wondering how best to share something from Scripture that would encourage, comfort or challenge. In those early pastoral visits most of the time I was so uptight I could hardly remember from one minute to the next what was said. Then I read something that changed all of that: if you want to get to know someone, try being curious. I tried it in the next pastoral visit. I asked clarifying questions regardless if they were about diesel engines, cats or a child struggling with a mental illness. I wanted to understand more. My curiosity made people feel heard and understood. Curiosity freed me to offer appropriate words from Scripture. It opened relationships by being a nonintrusive way to enter the lives of my parishioners. For me, curiosity proved to be a tipping point in my pastoral ministry.

We are often stuck in our relationships because we criticize, judge, blame, belittle or are apathetic. We are more condemning than curious. Instead of blaming our spouse, what if we were curious about why they are acting as they are and what is giving shape to their feelings? Instead of arguing with our teenagers, what if we were curious about the challenges they are facing? What if we were more curious about our own motivations? What if we were curious about the way we structured our emotional understanding of God? What if we were curious enough to read the Gospels and place ourselves in the events as we read them?

Relationships are always limited and restricted by our blaming and projecting. The latter is when we take our disowned interior agenda and displace it on another. Instead of curiosity we live from presumption. We tell others who they are, what they think, how they feel. This presumptuous arrogance restricts and narrows relational communion. Curiosity is the means to undermine our blaming and projecting. Be an explorer of the hearts of those you love. Be curious.

Curiosity proves to be an invitation for transformation. Inevitably, we will be invited to let go and to live into something more. Remember Zacchaeus, who climbed the tree to see Jesus? Where did his curiosity land him? So powerful was his encounter with Christ that he let go of old ways of living to embrace a life he never imagined. There probably weren't too many tax collectors so curious that they climbed trees to learn more about an itinerant preacher. But Zacchaeus did! He couldn't contain himself. He had to see more even if it meant going out on a limb (literally).

Curiosity is dangerous, but soulful relationships depend on it. If you are having difficulty in a relationship, we encourage you to practice a holy curiosity that explores the soul of another. It is a sad thing to think there is nothing more to understand about our soul or the souls of others. Climb out on a limb with curiosity and you just may be surprised at who sees you.

Acceptance of our limits and losses. Life is filled with incomplete symphonies. We have very real limits and losses that will not go away no matter what we do. A parent dies too soon. Mothers will never enjoy watching their daughters get married because of severe autism. Dads' sons will never come home. Young adults will always struggle over their lost childhood in a home where Dad was disinterested and Mom was preoccupied. Opportunities are missed because of limited perceptions or our own limited ability to embrace love. There are no magic wands to wave for these kinds of limits and losses.

We can rail against them in our anger and sadness, or we can learn to make peace with them after facing the emotions they invoke. Soulful relationships require the latter. We cannot engage well with others without accepting our limits and losses. If we stay angry or decide to live in our sadness, we allow the limits and losses to restrict us, to bind us, to narrow our capacity for love in life.

Unfortunately, many of us have not reconciled our souls to our limits and losses. We have never come to terms with the difficulties of our lives. Accepting our limits and our losses brings us home to ourselves. The way into this acceptance is through surrender, not attainment. It is through letting go, not holding on to what we wish life would have been. When our mothers died of cancer (Rich was twenty-four; Jim was forty-six) the loss could not be reversed. We had to learn to surrender and relinquish. Birthdays, family reunions, weddings, vacations and the birth of grandchildren now happen without them. It took years for each of us to make peace with our loss. In the meantime there were plenty of poor decisions made in reaction to our loss. But eventually the willingness to accept and relinquish has expanded, softened and deepened our souls. We have more clarity about what really matters.

It is impossible to live into soulful relationships while desperately clutching bitterness or resentment. When the soul is cluttered with these emotions, there isn't room for the real presence of others. In suffering our losses and limits the soul is recalibrated to see and understand what is truly real. This requires us to feel the pain of what will never be and accept what can never change. Ultimately, this can be done to the extent that we come to know and experience that our suffering is held by our suffering Christ. He does not remove our pain but is with us in it. He knows the experience of limits and losses better than we do.

Opening by faith to the presence of Christ in our pain opens our hearts to new possibilities and restrains the constricting powers of bitterness and resentment. The soul is simplified, and in this simplification there comes space for the presence of others. Coming to terms with our limits and losses opens us to be more receptive rather than reactive. Through our acceptance a contentment of soul arises. We become more welcoming and less afraid of life. Life is lived with a depth of awareness that is impossible except through accepting limits and suffering losses. In acceptance we learn that in dying we are born to life.

Forgiveness and beginning again. Accepting the limits and losses of our lives requires a lot of letting go. And there is no process of letting go that is harder than forgiveness. In forgiveness we let go of the retribution we are owed. In forgiveness we release others from the payment we deserve because of their actions or attitudes. In forgiveness we absorb the pain and the loss. That can be very difficult. But soulful relationships are impossible without forgiveness. With forgiveness we can begin again together.

In Christ God forgives us of our mistrust and distance. He releases us from the payment we owe for our failure to find our life in him. And as a result of the great gift of forgiveness we can begin again with God, ourselves and others. We accept his forgiveness as a gift we cannot earn. We accept this gift again and again, and so we begin again and again. Here we are back again to receiving, not achieving. We relinquish to a gift that is given. Our willingness to accept forgiveness and begin again is an act of obedience. In the ordinary routine of coming to know ourselves and our addictions we confess our weaknesses and sins and accept forgiveness.

Beginning again and again is steadfastness. In the steadfastness of making our way as forgiven children of God we begin to see the beauty of God. Our hearts yearn for more. So we begin again and again and again. This is the way home to ourselves. It is the way of transformation.

The acceptance of our forgiveness in Christ changes us. And when we give this gift to others, it will lead and sustain soulful relationships more than any one thing we can do. Forgiveness is a process, especially when it comes to the pain others have caused. Don't rush it. But stay with it. Soulful relationships depend on it.

BRINGING IT HOME TO OUR HEARTS

Years ago William Blake summarized human existence with these words: "We are put on earth a little space, that we might learn to bear the beams of love."[2] That is what we have been driving at in *The Relational Soul*. The first commandment is not "be right!" It is "love!" We are to love God and love our neighbor like ourselves. We are here to love, so our focus has been on how we learn to do it well. We can love because we live in God's love. The love of God in Christ is irrevocable, unshakeable and eternal. God has promised never to let us go. As Paul said, "Nothing in all creation will ever be able to separate us from the love of God that is revealed in Christ Jesus our Lord" (Romans 8:39).

Our lives are held in love forever by the Lord of heaven and earth. Here is where our journey of transformation begins, transpires and ends. Old habits die hard, but God's love endures forever. Grumpy, crabby, cantankerous attitudes are not easily shaken, but God's love endures forever. Anxiety, fear, guilt and shame hang on us like a sweaty T-shirt on a hot and humid day, but God's love endures forever. Lingering memories of abuse, brokenness and even hatred haunt the soul, but God's love endures forever. We rest in God's love, and in his love we are transformed. We live bearing the beams of God's love. Change is anchored in this love, and so too are the soulful relationships that all true transformation serves.

There was no story at the beginning of this chapter as there was in each of the others. That was by design. This chapter needs *your* story! The good, the bad, the ugly. The highs and lows. The joys and disappointments. All of your story needs to be told and heard. You matter to God. And you matter to others. May God grant you the wisdom, strength and courage to live more fully alive in your true self. Amen.

For Reflection and Discussion

1. Do you feel that significant change is possible for you? Why or why not? What would you like to see changed in your way of relating to God, others and yourself?

2. Do you resonate with the statement "Change is possible, but it is harder than we want and takes longer than we expect"? Will you explain from your experience why or why not that is true for you?

3. What do you think of the five characteristics of receptivity considered in this chapter? How have they proved to be life giving in your life?

4. How might you become more openhearted? More attentive?

5. How might you become more curious? More forgiving?

6. Are there limits and losses that need to be reconciled in your soul? If so, name them.

7. What most strikes you about *The Relational Soul*? Why? Are you willing to take the next step to relational health? If so, turn to page 186.

ACKNOWLEDGMENTS

ﾉ

*C*rossPoint exists because of the generous and loving encouragement of numerous friends. We are deeply grateful for each one of you. Special thanks goes to our dear friend Eric Johnson, who always has another book for us to read, and for our times of prayer together at Abbey of Gethsemane. And to Leigh Conver and Steve Macchia who encouraged us to put our thoughts in writing. Jim and Barbara McQuire, Don and Debbie Seefeldt, Dick and Nora Lewis, Richard Persons, Arnie and Sue Steeves, George and Lori Griffiths, Bob and Charlotte Canida, Mark and Arlene Smith, David and Beth Hussung, Cheri Skorupa, Tony and Sandy Fiacchino, Bill and Kathryne Oates, Don and Cheryl Voss, and Jim and Ceecy Abrahamson have helped us pursue our calling to care for the souls of Christian leaders.

We are also thankful for the input and refinement of our thoughts that came from the pastors and staffs of Grace Community Church, Noblesville, Indiana; Sojourn Community Church, Louisville, Kentucky; Savannah Christian Church,

Savannah, Georgia; Harvester Christian Church, St. Charles, Missouri; Living Stones Church, Reno, Nevada; as well as hundreds of other leaders and friends around the country.

Appendix One

ADDITIONAL READING

MANY HAVE INFLUENCED OUR THINKING on the matter of relationships. The following is a list of some authors we have found helpful. While not endorsing all of what these authors say we offer this list for additional reading.

Chapter 1: Our Relational Reality

Boersma, Hans. *Heavenly Participation: The Weaving of a Sacramental Tapestry*. Grand Rapids: Eerdmans, 2011.

Fairbairn, Donald. *Life in the Trinity: An Introduction to Theology with the Help of the Church Fathers*. Downers Grove, IL: IVP Academic, 2010.

Johnson, Eric. *Foundations of Soul Care: A Christian Psychology Proposal*. Downers Grove, IL: IVP Academic, 2009.

Meek, Esther Lightcap. *Loving to Know: Covenant Epistemology*. Eugene, OR: Cascade, 2011.

Reeves, Michael. *Delighting in the Trinity: An Introduction to the Christian Faith*. Downers Grove, IL: IVP Academic, 2012.

Torrance, James B. *Worship, Community and the Triune God of Grace*. Downers Grove, IL: IVP Academic, 1997.

Chapter 2: Attachment

Clinton, Tim, and Gary Sibcy. *Attachments: Why You Love, Feel and Act the Way You Do*. Nashville: Nelson, 2009.

Friedman, Edwin H. *Generation to Generation: Family Process in Church and Synagogue*. New York: Guilford, 2011.

Karen, Robert. *Becoming Attached: First Relationships and How They Shape Our Capacity to Love*. New York: Oxford University Press, 1998.

Siegel, Daniel J. *The Developing Mind: How Relationships and the Brain Interact to Shape Who We Are*. 2nd ed. New York: Guilford, 2012.

Chapter 3: Memory

Coe, John, and Todd Hall. *Psychology in the Spirit: Contours of a Transformational Psychology*. Downers Grove, IL: IVP Academic, 2010.

Siegel, Daniel J. *Mindsight: The New Science of Personal Transformation*. New York: Bantam, 2010.

Stump, Eleonore. *Wandering in Darkness: Narratives and the Problem of Suffering*. New York: Oxford University Press, 2012. See chapter three for a distinction between Dominican (head) and Franciscan (heart) ways of knowing.

Chapter 4: The Reactive False Self

Benner, David G. *The Gift of Being Yourself*. Downers Grove, IL: IVP Books, 2004.

Canlis, Julie. *Calvin's Ladder: A Spiritual Theology of Ascent and Ascension*. Grand Rapids: Eerdmans, 2010.

Capps, Donald. *The Depleted Self: Sin in a Narcissistic Age*. Minneapolis: Fortress Press, 1993.

Hotchkiss, Sandy. *Why Is It Always About You? The Seven Deadly Sins of Narcissism*. New York: Free Press, 2003.

May, Gerald. *Addiction and Grace: Love and Spirituality in the Healing of Addiction*. New York: HarperOne, 1991.

Merton, Thomas. *New Seeds of Contemplation*. Rev. ed. New York: New Directions, 1972.

Mulholland, M. Robert, Jr. *The Deeper Journey: The Spirituality of Discovering Your True Self*. Downers Grove, IL: IVP Books, 2012.

Owen, John. *Mortification of Sin*. London: Banner of Truth, 2004.

Pennington, M. Basil. *True Self/False Self: Unmasking the Spirit Within*. New York: Crossroad, 2000.

Chapter 5: Gift of Grace

Boulton, Matthew Myer. *Life in God: John Calvin, Practical Formation, and the Future of Protestant Theology*. Grand Rapids: Eerdmans, 2011.

Campbell, Constantine R. *Paul and Union with Christ: An Exegetical and Theological Study*. Grand Rapids: Zondervan, 2012.

Canlis, Julie. *Calvin's Ladder: A Spiritual Theology of Ascent and Ascension*. Grand Rapids: Eerdmans, 2010.

Casey, Michael. *Athirst for God: Spiritual Desire in Bernard of Clairvaux's Sermons on the Song of Songs*. Collegeville, MN: Cistercian Publications, 1988.

Humphrey, Edith. *Ecstasy and Intimacy: When the Holy Spirit Meets the Human Spirit*. Grand Rapids: Eerdmans, 2005.

Lane, Belden C. *Ravished by Beauty: The Surprising Legacy of Reformed Spirituality*. New York: Oxford University Press, 2011.

Letham, Robert. *Union with Christ: In Scripture, History, and Theology*. Phillipsburg, NJ: P&R, 2011.

Roberts, Robert C., and Mark R. Talbot. *Limning the Psyche: Explorations in Christian Psychology*. Grand Rapids: Eerdmans, 1997.

Schwanda, Tom. *Soul Recreation: The Contemplative-Mystical Piety of Puritanism*. Eugene, OR: Wipf & Stock, 2012.

Tozer, A. W. *The Divine Conquest*. Harrisburg, PA: Christian Publications, 1950.

Chapter 6: The Receptive True Self

Behr, John. *The Mystery of Christ: Life in Death*. Yonkers, NY: St. Vladimir's Seminary Press, 2006.

Benner, David G. *Surrender to Love: Discovering the Heart of Christian Spirituality*. Downers Grove, IL: IVP Books, 2003.

Billings, J. Todd. *Union with Christ: Reframing Theology and Ministry for the Church*. Grand Rapids: Baker, 2011.

Gifford, James D., Jr. *Perichoretic Salvation: The Believer's Union with Christ as a Third Type of* Perichoresis. Eugene, OR: Wipf & Stock, 2011.

Grenz, Stanley J. *The Social God and the Relational Self: A Trinitarian Theology of the Imago Dei*. Louisville: Westminster John Knox, 2007.

Haase, Albert. *Coming Home to Your True Self*. Downers Grove, IL: IVP Books, 2008.

Jones, Alan. *Soul Making: The Desert Way of Spirituality*. New York: HarperOne, 1989.

Mulholland, M. Robert, Jr. *The Deeper Journey: The Spirituality of Discovering Your True Self*. Downers Grove, IL: IVP Books, 2012.

Chapter 7: Self-Understanding

Baron, Renee, and Elizabeth Wagele. *Are You My Type, Am I Yours?* New York: HarperOne, 1995.

———. *The Enneagram Made Easy*. New York: HarperOne, 1994.

Gilbert, Roberta M. *Extraordinary Relationships: A New Way of Thinking About Human Interactions*. New York: Wiley, 1992.

Riso, Don Richardson, and Russ Hudson. *The Wisdom of the Enneagram: The Complete Guide to Psychological and Spiritual Growth for the Nine Personality Types*. New York: Bantam, 1999.

Rohr, Richard, and Andreas Ebert. *The Enneagram: A Christian Perspective*. New York: Crossroad, 2001.

Thompson, Curt. *Anatomy of the Soul: Surprising Connections Between Neuroscience and Spiritual Practices That Can Transform Your Life and Relationships*. Carol Stream, IL: Tyndale Momentum, 2010.

Wagner, Jerome. *The Enneagram Spectrum of Personality: An Introductory Guide*. Evanston, IL: Enneagram Studies and Applications, 1996.

Chapter 8: Community

Bonhoeffer, Dietrich. *Life Together: A Discussion of Christian Fellowship*. New York: HarperOne, 2009.

Crabb, Larry. *Connecting: A Radical New Vision*. Nashville: Thomas Nelson, 1997.

———. *The Safest Place on Earth: Where People Connect and Are Changed Forever*. Nashville: Thomas Nelson, 1999.

Edwards, Jonathan. *Charity and Its Fruits: Living in the Light of God's Love*. Edited by Kyle Strobel. Wheaton, IL: Crossway, 2012.

Gilbert, Roberta M. *The Eight Concepts of Bowen Theory: A New Way of Thinking About the Individual and the Group*. Falls Church, VA: Leading Systems, 2006.

Solomon, Marion. *Lean on Me: The Power of Positive Dependency in Intimate Relationships*. New York: Simon & Schuster, 1994.

Chapter 9: Core Spiritual Disciplines

Balthasar, Hans Urs von. *Engagement with God: The Drama of Christian Discipleship*. San Francisco: Ignatius Press, 2008.

Benner, David G. *Opening to God: Lectio Divina and Life as Prayer*. Downers Grove, IL: IVP Books, 2010.

Bourgeault, Cynthia. *Centering Prayer and Inner Awakening*. Lanham, MD: Cowley, 2004.

Buchanan, Mark. *Spiritual Rhythm: Being with Jesus Every Season of Your Soul*. Grand Rapids: Zondervan, 2010.

Casey, Michael. *Sacred Reading: The Ancient Art of Lectio Divina*. Liguori, MO: LiguoriTriumph, 1997.

———. *Toward God: The Ancient Wisdom of Western Prayer*. Rev. ed. Liguori, MO: LiguoriTriumph, 1996.

Davis, John Jefferson. *Meditation and Communion with God: Contemplating Scripture in an Age of Distraction*. Downers Grove, IL: IVP Academic, 2012.

Issler, Klaus. *Wasting Time with God: A Christian Spirituality of Friendship with God*. Downers Grove, IL: IVP Books, 2001.

Merton, Thomas. *The Inner Experience: Notes on Contemplation*. San Francisco: HarperSanFrancisco, 2004.

Mulholland, M. Robert, Jr. *Shaped by the Word: The Power of Scripture in Spiritual Formation*. Rev. ed. Nashville: Upper Room, 2001.

Sanders, J. Oswald. *Enjoying Intimacy with God*. Grand Rapids: Discovery House, 2000.

Tozer, A. W. *The Pursuit of God*. Ventura, CA: Regal, 2013.

Willard, Dallas. *Hearing God: Developing a Conversational Relationship with God*. Updated ed. Downers Grove, IL: IVP Books, 2012.

Chapter 10: Transformation

Ford, Leighton. *The Attentive Life: Discerning God's Presence in All Things*. Downers Grove, IL: IVP Books, 2008.

Gire, Ken. *The Reflective Life: Becoming More Spiritually Sensitive to the Everyday Moments of Life*. Colorado Springs: Chariot Victor, 1998.

Kendall, R. T. *Total Forgiveness*. London: Hodder & Stoughton, 2001.

Kruger, C. Baxter. *The Great Dance: The Christian Vision Revisited*. Jackson, MS: Perichoresis, 2008.

Lewis, C. S. *The Problem of Pain*. New York: HarperOne, 2009.

Lynch, John, Bruce McNicol and Bill Thrall. *The Cure: What If God Isn't Who You Think He Is and Neither Are You?* Colorado Springs: NavPress, 2011.

MAKING A LIFE MAP

THERE ARE MANY HELPFUL RESOURCES available when it comes to unpacking your story (for example, *Life Mapping* by John Trent; *To Be Told: God Invites You to Coauthor Your Future* by Dan B. Allender; storylineblog.com). But all you need to get started is a few sheets of paper. In the top third of the page record the events you remember, in the middle third record the emotions you felt surrounding the events, and in the bottom third write the interpretation that you may have made. For example:

Event: My dog was killed by a car.

Emotion: Very sad.

Interpretation: I'm not going to get another dog.

> or
>
> I'm not going to get too close to anyone because it hurts if they go away. [This interpretation may be the culmination of many painful events.]

We invite you to consider what you have lived. Start a life map by recording important memories as far back as you can. Don't be frustrated with the gaps in your memory. God will help you recall what is needed for healing and health when the time is right. After you have a couple of pages of memories you can begin to think about how the events shaped you. How were you influenced and formed by what you experienced? It doesn't need to be a long explanation. The point is simply trying to be clear on who you have become in light of what you lived. Finally, take a look at what you see at the present time. See if you can identify habitual patterns that make you who you are. In addition to behaviors, pay attention to the habits of thought and patterns of feelings. Are there are enduring patterns reaching into how you live now?

In this exercise we are attempting to have you intentionally reflect on your own story—what formed it, how you think of yourself and the habitual way you go about being you at the present time. All of what you have lived—the good, the bad, the ugly—is held in God ("For you died to this life, and your real life is hidden with Christ in God" [Colossians 3:3]). Nothing we have lived is outside the view of God or the presence of God. Are there painful things? Certainly. For some there have been very painful, even traumatic, events. What many have endured grieves God. But the gospel story says God was with you in your suffering.

Reflection fosters an integration of all that we lived within ourselves and within God's presence. We simply *must* own our story because w*hatever we disown will in some way own us*. The more you can express and experience your story through life mapping the better. What you have lived matters!

WHAT WE REMEMBER

The reason you remember an event is because of its emotional impact on your soul. A spectacular idea is registered in our conscious memory because it is attended by an emotion. In other words no one remembers just an idea. We remember because of an emotion that implicit memory has attached to the event. The events we remember from our childhood are about encounters with others. We remember the experiences because of their emotional impact for good or ill.

For example, I (Rich) remember Gary, my childhood buddy, getting punched in the mouth by George sometime around fifth grade. Gary went home crying, and I followed. The first person we ran into was Gary's father. He looked at Gary's mouth and asked if he lost any teeth. While Gary sobbed and shook his head no, his father said something to the effect that Gary needed to learn to be a man because life can hit you in the mouth from time to time. Now, I have no idea of the neurotic consequences in Gary's soul from this encounter with George's fist or his father's interpretation of life. But I remember this event, out of thousands of events in my childhood, because of its emotional impact on me. I'm certain Gary does as well!

When you explore your memories and your interpretation of them, it is crucial to pay attention to the emotions that come into awareness. Joy, excitement, anxiety, pain, shame, fear, hope, sadness and guilt are a few of the common emotions embedded in the interpretation of events. We must pay attention to the emotions because they have given shape to our understanding of ourselves. Emotions affect our interpretation, and our interpretation is a way by which we explain ourselves and relate to others. So a careful and thoughtful exploration of our remembered events can bring insight into the early emotional orientation of our soul. By understanding our story we begin to see what emotions are shaping our current relationships.

GETTING HELP WITH OUR INTERPRETATIONS

Because our emotions can be confusing, we need help in reconciling what we feel with the realities of life. We need the voice of others to reassure us that we are safe, that we have what it takes to succeed, that we can do what is needed. In other words, we need the healthy and appropriate input of others to help us interpret our own lives well. We are dependent on mature people around us to provide us with an accurate assessment of what we experienced so that our interpretation is sound and true, congruent with reality. But the fact that we need others means we are vulnerable to the interpretation of others. Children especially have a limited capacity for assessing life accurately. They are great observers but poor interpreters.

The interpretation Gary got from his father of his run-in with George could not have been helpful! I can remember thinking, *Don't you care that your son's mouth is bleeding?* For me, something was incongruent with his dad's response. It wasn't a true assessment of the reality of a father's love for his son. I'm sure Gary felt that. But if you hear crazy interpretations long enough as a kid, you wind up believing them.

Ideas certainly have consequences when it comes to healing our interpretations. But what is needed at the core of our being in order for our implicit memory to shift from mistrust to trust, from reactivity to receptivity, is a great story heard repeatedly—a story of good overcoming evil, of God becoming man, of death and resurrection, of descending and ascending, of surrender and hope—a story personified since we are relational at our core.

In other words each of us needs the presence of another to bear witness to *the* story that meets us at the deepest terrain of our soul. *The* story is earthy enough, powerful enough, real enough, honest enough and loving enough to hold every detail of our story. When our soul is greeted by this story through the loving presence of another, the interpretation of our life can change, and with that, the way we relate to God and others.

Appendix Three

An Overview
of the Enneagram

THE ENNEAGRAM IS A TOOL that identifies nine ways of *presenting* ourselves to others (nine personality styles). The nine styles are divided into triads (Heart, Head, Gut). The triads indicate our ways of *perceiving* and *processing*. Each triad, like each style, has particular strengths and challenges associated with it (see table 2). Each also has a primary emotion that can be either exaggerated or diminished, affecting the way we perceive, process and present ourselves. To the extent we are unaware of how the emotion is at work, we will manage it in ways that are not healthy.

Table 2. The Enneagram

Style	Resourceful	Nonresourceful
Heart Triad (*perceive* reality in terms of connections to be made; *process* with feelings; *present* themselves very relationally; underlying emotion is *shame*)		
Two	• Loving, Helpful • Healthy boundaries	• Enmeshed • Codependent
Three	• Efficient, Socially skilled • Successful	• Manipulative • Image oriented
Four	• Original, Dynamic • Authentic	• Melancholy, Isolated • Exaggerated sensitivity

Head Triad (*perceive* reality in terms of finding a safe place; *process* with cognition; *present* themselves as having things figured out; underlying emotion is *fear*)		
Five	• Wise, Objective • Thinker, Summarizer	• Detached, Greedy • Don't trust
Six	• Reliable, Committed • Loyal, Traditional	• Anxiety, Fear • Paranoid
Seven	• Fun-loving • Spontaneous	• Impulsive, Scattered • Random escapism
Gut Triad (*perceive* reality as against them; *process* with intuition; *present* themselves as grounded in the present situation; underlying emotion is *guilt*)		
Eight	• Energy, Power • Pushing forward	• Demanding, Unaware • Emotional bulldozer
Nine	• Harmonious • Cooperation	• Passive, Paralyzed • Control through being a victim
One	• Reforming • Change agent for good	• Perfectionist, Legalistic • Nonresilient

There are many enneagram profiles available. The one we use gives a numerical rating of both the strengths (resourceful aspects) and challenges (nonresourceful aspects) of each of the nine styles. You can take the profile (and receive a consultation if you so desire) by going to our website at crosspointministry.com.

A Guide for
Group Discussion

Healthy relationships are the lifeblood of the soul.
Most participants in a group will naturally long for better relationships. So the topic of this book is user friendly. However,
getting to the root of our capacity for significant relationships
is often challenging. Exaggerated shame, fear and guilt work
to undermine the best of desires for connecting. Some level of
mistrust is alive and well in all of us. That affects our willingness to share all of our story. We doubt whether there is
sufficient safety and grace to hold all of who we are and have
done. And in some groups that may be the case. But without
being honest with ourselves about what we have lived, without
the embrace of community and the confidence that God is for
us, we will find it hard to change.

The key to more relational heath is healthy relationships. In
other words, we need people around us who model what it
means to connect well. Groups can be a big part of the healing
process if there are participants who have done good soul

work. Clearly, a group that nurtures healing and health cannot be manufactured. It grows over time when it is clear to all that the group is safe.

If you have been in a group over an extended period of time, sharing the ups and downs of life, this book could be used as a ten-week conversation guide for each participant.

1. Read the assigned chapter before the group meets. Write your responses to the questions at the end of the chapter. Take note of the question that resonates with you most. Come to the group willing to share why that is the case.

2. Start the group discussion with each participant answering

   • What struck me most from the chapter?

   • Why do I think that is the case?

3. Continue the discussion answering

   • How has my sin (what I've done) or suffering (what's been done to me) or both contributed to this matter?

   • What might God's invitation be to me in light of what I'm discovering about myself?

4. Explore specific ways that the group can encourage each member of the group (affirming God's love, asking what someone wants to do about what they are discovering, etc.).

5. Commit yourselves to God in prayer for yourself and for your fellow group members before you leave. Then pray for each person each day for the one issue he or she is addressing.

If you are just starting a group, we suggest that the members be encouraged to go slowly in light of the following guidelines.

1. Ask each participant to commit to absolute confidentiality. The capacity to trust well is at the heart of nurturing relationships. Developing the capacity for trust takes place only in the context of safety. Since trust is crucial, the commitment from each member must be verbal and made to the entire group.

2. Remind the group of the heart of the gospel—God is for us. God makes it safe for us to stop running from him. He longs for us to draw near in order to experience his rich mercy and grace. We can trust him with our stories.

3. Encourage participants to disclose only what they feel comfortable sharing. While we long to be loved in order to love, we are fallen creatures who tend to doubt whether there is a love that can hold all of who we are and what we have lived.

4. Resist the impulse to fix others with declarations. Instead, encourage a spirit of discovery. People take ownership of their lives when they discern the decisions needed for transformation. Trust the Holy Spirit to bring about transformation in their lives through your loving presence.

5. Remember that no matter how difficult and discouraging the details of someone's story are, the desire motivating every individual is the pursuit of life-giving relationships. The invitation from Christ in the gospel is to find our greatest source of well-being in him.

Notes

Chapter 1: Our Relational Reality

[1]Henri J. M. Nouwen, *Reaching Out: The Three Movements of the Spiritual Life* (New York: Image Books, 1975), p. 24.

[2]See Esther Lightcap Meek, *Loving to Know: Covenant Epistemology* (Eugene, OR: Cascade, 2011) for a convincing case that all reality and thus all knowing is relational and thus interpersonal.

Chapter 3: Memory

[1]The following two paragraphs rely on the work of John H. Coe and Todd W. Hall, *Psychology in the Spirit: Contours of a Transformational Psychology* (Downers Grove, IL: InterVarsity Press, 2010), pp. 236-39. They describe implicit memory as a "gut memory" in that it contributes to an instinctual way of knowing.

[2]Daniel J. Siegel, *The Developing Mind: How Relationships and the Brain Interact to Shape Who We Are* (New York: Guilford Press, 1999), p. 29.

[3]Coe and Hall, *Psychology in the Spirit*, p. 239.

[4]Ibid., p. 241.

[5]Ibid., p. 242.

[6]Much of our understanding of emotional blueprints rests on the work of Susan M. Johnson, *The Practice of Emotionally Focused Couples Therapy*, 2nd ed. (New York: Brunner-Routledge, 2004), pp. 41-52.

[7]See Siegel, *Developing Mind*, chap. 4.

Chapter 4: The Reactive False Self

[1]See Eleonore Stump, *Wandering in Darkness: Narratives and the Problem of Suffering* (Oxford: Clarendon Press, 2010), pp. 129-50.

[2]For an exposition of sin's essential narcissistic, self-centered structure see Cornelius Plantinga, *Not the Way It's Suppose to Be: A Breviary of Sin* (Grand Rapids: Eerdmans, 1995); and Christopher Lasch, *The Culture of Narcissism: American Life in an Age of Diminishing Expectations* (New York: W. W. Norton, 1979).

[3]For example, "Paul's 'flesh life' is the pervasively self-referenced life of the false self," in Robert Mulholland, *The Deeper Journey: The Spirituality of Discovering Your True Self* (Downers Grove, IL: InterVarsity Press, 2006), p. 42.

[4]John Calvin, *Institutes of the Christian Religion* 1.1.1, Library of Christian Classics, ed. John T. McNeill, trans. Ford Lewis Battles (Philadelphia: Westminster Press, 1960), 1:35.

CHAPTER 5: GIFT OF GRACE

[1]Julie Canlis, *Calvin's Ladder: A Spiritual Theology of Ascent and Ascension* (Grand Rapids: Eerdmans, 2010), p. 8.

[2]Edith Humphrey, *Ecstasy and Intimacy: When the Holy Spirit Meets the Human Spirit* (Grand Rapids: Eerdmans, 2006), p. 4.

[3]Dietrich Bonhoeffer, *The Cost of Discipleship* (New York: Macmillan, 1963), p. 97.

CHAPTER 6: THE RECEPTIVE TRUE SELF

[1]David Benner, *The Gift of Being Yourself: The Sacred Call to Self-Discovery* (Downers Grove, IL: InterVarsity Press, 2004), p. 91.

[2]Henri J. M. Nouwen, *Reaching Out: The Three Movements of the Spiritual Life* (New York: Image Books, 1975), p. 51.

CHAPTER 7: SELF-UNDERSTANDING

[1]Alan E. Lewis, *Between Cross and Resurrection: A Theology of Holy Saturday* (Grand Rapids: Eerdmans, 2001), p. 192.

[2]Timothy Keller, *The Reason for God: Belief in an Age of Skepticism* (New York: Penguin, 2008), p. 32.

[3]John Calvin, *Institutes of the Christian Religion* 1.1.1, Library of Christian Classics, ed. John T. McNeill, trans. Ford Lewis Battles (Philadelphia: Westminster Press, 1960), 1:35.

Chapter 8: Community

[1]Thomas Merton, *No Man Is an Island* (New York: Barnes & Noble, 2003), p. xii.

[2]Dietrich Bonhoeffer, *Life Together: A Discussion of Christian Fellowship* (New York: Harper & Row, 1954), p. 27.

[3]Gregory Jones, *Embodying Forgiveness: A Theological Analysis* (Grand Rapids: Eerdmans, 1995), p. xiii.

[4]Alan Jones and John O'Neil, *Seasons of Grace* (Hoboken, NJ: John Wiley, 2003), p. 3.

Chapter 9: Core Spiritual Disciplines

[1]Spiritual disciplines include worship, study, journaling, spiritual friendships, service and fasting, just to name a few. We encourage you to review Adele Calhoun's book *Spiritual Disciplines Handbook: Practices That Transform Us* (Downers Grove, IL: InterVarsity Press, 2005) for a comprehensive list.

[2]In *Loving to Know: Covenant Epistemology* (Eugene, OR: Cascade, 2011), Esther Lightcap Meeks explains how coming to know anything is an interpersonal enterprise dependent on love (see especially pp. 3-64).

[3]Henri J. M. Nouwen, *The Only Necessary Thing: Living a Prayerful Life* (New York: Crossroad, 1999), p. 35.

Chapter 10: Transformation

[1]Leighton Ford, *The Attentive Life: Discerning God's Presence in All Things* (Downers Grove, IL: InterVarsity Press, 2008), p. 25.

[2]William Blake, quoted in Gerald May, *The Awakened Heart: Opening Yourself to the Love You Need* (San Francisco: HarperSanFrancisco, 1991), p. 1.

RESOURCES FROM
CrossPoint

*Are you ready to take the next step
toward a relational soul?*

As an Individual
1. Connect with us:
   - crosspointministry.com
   - facebook.com/crosspointministry
   - Twitter: @crosspointmin
2. Take the profile (get a nearly 50% discount by using the code **book50**):
   - crosspointministry.com/enneagram-profile

As a Leader of an Organization
1. Have your staff take the profile:
   - Contact us at profile@crosspointministry.com for information.
2. Sponsor a *Relational Soul retreat:*
   - Contact us at info@crosspointministry.com for information.

Our Approach to Christian Spiritual Formation
- Biblically based—We believe Scripture presents a full-orbed understanding of the human condition and God's provision for life.
- Historically informed—We believe the wisdom of God's people in the past gives us insight into the nature of the soul's transformation.
- Psychologically sensitive—We believe spiritual maturity is impossible without healthy development of the soul.
- Relationally focused—We believe the soul is formed and transformed through relational participation in and with Christ, the transformed and transforming presence of others, and Christian spiritual disciplines.

formatio
TRADITION. EXPERIENCE.
TRANSFORMATION.

Formatio books from InterVarsity Press follow the rich tradition of the church in the journey of spiritual formation. These books are not merely about being informed, but about being transformed by Christ and conformed to his image. Formatio stands in InterVarsity Press's evangelical publishing tradition by integrating God's Word with spiritual practice and by prompting readers to move from inward change to outward witness. InterVarsity Press uses the chambered nautilus for Formatio, a symbol of spiritual formation because of its continual spiral journey outward as it moves from its center. We believe that each of us is made with a deep desire to be in God's presence. Formatio books help us to fulfill our deepest desires and to become our true selves in light of God's grace.